Water in Southern Africa

OFF-CENTRE

NEW PERSPECTIVES ON PUBLIC ISSUES

Series editors: John Higgins, Kole Omotoso and Peter Vale

OFF-CENTRE is a book series focused on the social, political and cultural life of South Africa and the southern African region. The series offers new perspectives on issues of public interest and concern. Written in a deliberately accessible style, each book presents an engaging and informative read for specialist and lay-person alike, utilising the best of academic scholarship to challenge and correct conventional wisdoms.

Volume 1: *Water in Southern Africa* by Larry A. Swatuk

OFF-CENTRE

NEW PERSPECTIVES ON PUBLIC ISSUES

VOLUME 1

Water in Southern Africa

Larry A. Swatuk

UI
KZN
PRESS UNIVERSITY OF KWAZULU-NATAL PRESS

Published in 2017 by University of KwaZulu-Natal Press
Private Bag X01
Scottsville, 3209
Pietermaritzburg
South Africa
Email: books@ukzn.ac.za
Website: www.ukznpress.co.za

ISBN: 978 1 86914 364 0
e-ISBN: 978 1 86914 365 7

Managing editor: Sally Hines
Editor: Sean Fraser
Typesetter: Patricia Comrie
Proofreader: Christopher Merrett
Cover design: Marise Bauer, M Design
Cover image: Richard Human / Independent Contributors / Africa Media Online

Print administration by DJE Flexible Print Solutions, Cape Town

Contents

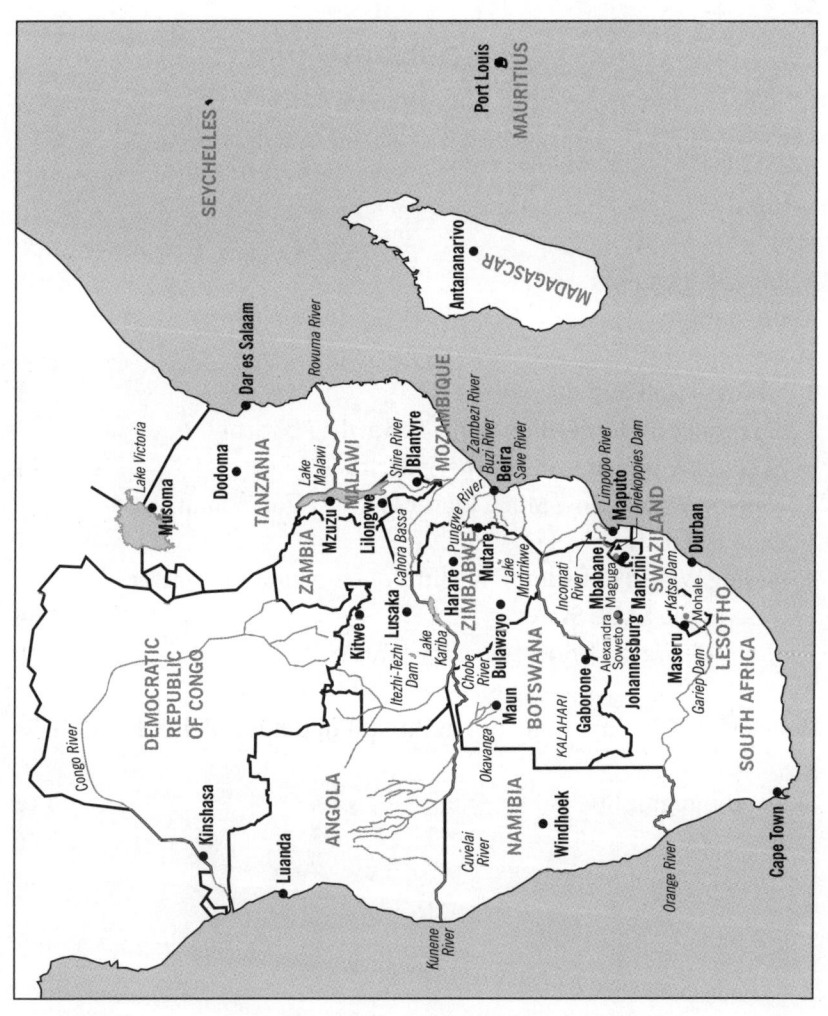

This book is dedicated to the memory of
Lewis Jonker,
teacher, friend, inspiration.

Acknowledgements

There is a great deal said about 'voice' and 'authenticity' in writing about people, places and things. So, I suppose, viewed one way, I'm just another Western white man 'writing' southern Africa. This is, of course, true. But, just as it is a mistake to lump the continent together as if it were an undifferentiated whole readily understandable to all, so, too, is it a mistake to simply call me – and perhaps, too, dismiss me – as just another *mzungu*.

In my mind, my Africa includes me, in part because of my 32-year association with the continent; but more centrally because my Africa consists of people united in a common humanity, divided though we are by categories of class, race, ethnicity, gender, age and so on. I was raised as a member of the working class, by immigrants of peasant stock who made their way in the so-called 'new world', first as hard-scrabble farmers or members of the service sector and, later, by their descendants who ultimately worked as tavern owners on the banks of the Detroit River. These were, of course, my grandparents and parents, to whom I owe an unfathomable debt of gratitude for the world they opened up to me.

It is something of a paradox that, while united by the mutual need for water and land and the sustenance these two resources bring, we are divided by the specificities of 'culture' that emerge out of different climatological settings, that is the myriad ways in which hydrology and landscape vary around the world. Three decades of working on water across varied landscapes has nevertheless revealed our common humanity to me, and illustrated quite clearly what is possible when we begin from a point of likeness rather than from a point of difference; at minimum it opens up a world of possibility for mutual learning and respect.

The water world in southern Africa is therefore global and local, collaborative and combative, united and divided, and this, in my view, is a good thing. Let us keep the conversation going. Let us listen attentively and be willing to shift our positions as new information reveals interests better understood. We have much to learn from each other.

There are so many people who have helped me see the water world differently, adding nuance and complexity, forcing me sometimes to dig up and discard fairly deeply rooted positions. Among these many people, I must thank first and foremost three Peters: Peter Vale, Pieter van der Zaag and Piet Heyns. You have taught me so much. I hope this little book does some justice to your faith in me. Second, I acknowledge the central contribution to my education of the region by my colleagues at the University of Botswana – especially those at the Okavango Research Institute – and the University of the Western Cape (UWC) in South Africa. I also thank my friends and colleagues working in important and lively regional organisations: CapNet, WaterNet, the GWP-SA, IWMI, the Water Research Commission-SA and SADC. These are hotbeds of scholarship, policy and planning that bring the local together with the global.

I also acknowledge the important contribution of my many students who have taught me as much as I have taught them. In particular, my long-running course on water and security, taught first at UWC and now also at the University of Waterloo in Canada, has provided an important venue for mutual learning and the exchange of ideas.

I wish to acknowledge, too, the financial contributions of the MacArthur Foundation and the University of Waterloo, which helped me bring fragmented thoughts together in what I hope is a coherent whole over the course of several years.

Lastly, I thank my spouse and best friend, Dr Corrine Cash, without whose unflagging support and limitless curiosity for the world none of this would be possible.

Abbreviations

AfDB	African Development Bank
AMCOW	African Ministerial Council on Water
ARWR	available renewable water resources
AU	African Union
AusAID	Australian Aid
BMZ	Bundesministerium für wirtschaftliche Zusammenarbeit (Federal Ministry for Economic Co-operation and Development, Germany)
CAR	Central African Republic
CBD	Central Business District
CGIAR	Consortium Group on International Agricultural Research
CMAs	Catchment Management Agencies
COMESA	Common Market of Eastern and Southern Africa
COP21	Twenty-first Convention of the Parties
DANIDA	Danish International Development Assistance
DBSA	Development Bank of Southern Africa
DfID	Department for International Development (United Kingdom)
DRC	Democratic Republic of Congo
DWA	Department of Water Affairs
ECOWAS	Economic Community of West African States
ELMS	Environment and Land Management Sector
EU	European Union

GDP	gross domestic product
GIZ	Deutche Gesellschaft für Internationale Zusammenarbeit (German Corporation for International Development)
GNI	Gross National Income
GW	gigawatt
GWP	Global Water Partnership
HDI	Human Development Index
HIV/AIDS	Human Immunodeficiency Virus/Acquired Immune Deficiency Syndrome
ICT	Information and Communications Technology
IGAD	Intergovernmental Authority on Development
IGOs	Intergovernmental Organisations
ILA	International Law Association
I-MTPTC	Inco-Maputo Tripartite Permanent Technical Committee
IPCC	Intergovernmental Panel on Climate Change
ITCZ	Inter-Tropical Convergence Zone
IWMI	International Water Management Institute
IWRM	Integrated Water Resources Management
JPTC	Joint Permanent Technical Committee
LBPTC	Limpopo Basin Permanent Technical Committee
LHDC	Lesotho Highlands Development Commission
LHWP	Lesotho Highlands Water Project
LIMCOM	Limpopo River Basin Commission
MCM	million cubic metres
MDGs	Millennium Development Goals
NGOs	non-governmental organisations
NORAD	Norwegian Aid
OECD	Organisation for Economic Co-operation and Development
OKACOM	Okavango River Basin Commission
ORASECOM	Orange-Senqu River Basin Commission
ORI	Okavango Research Institute

PJTC	Permanent Joint Technical Committee
PPCP	public-private-community partnership
PPP	public-private partnership
RBA	River Basin Authority
RBOs	River Basin Organisations
RSAP	Regional Strategic Action Plan
SADC	Southern African Development Community
SADCC	Southern African Development Co-ordination Conference
SIDA	Swedish International Development Assistance
SIDS	small island developing states
SIWI	Stockholm International Water Institute
TAZARA	Tanzania-Zambia Railway
TCTA	Trans-Caledon Tunnel Authority
TINA	There Is No Alternative
UKaid	United Kingdom Aid
UN	United Nations
UNC	United Nations Convention (on the Law of Non-Navigational Uses of International Watercourses)
UNDP	United Nations Development Programme
UNEP	United Nations Environment Programme
UNFPA	United Nations Population Fund
USAID	United States Agency for International Development
WaterNet	Water Network (of Southern Africa)
WB	World Bank
WWDR	World Water Development Report
ZAMCOM	Zambezi Basin Watercourse Commission
ZRA	Zambezi River Authority

1

A Glass Half Full

Water is life: true, but in many places the vitality of this connection is invisible. So plentiful is the resource, and so effective are the systems of delivery, that water is simply taken for granted. Flooding, drought, point-source and diffuse pollution, water-main breaks, sewerage back-up, even several deaths from defective potable water systems are routinised through the discourse of 'management' and the need to further improve existing systems. Where water is truly scarce – either seasonally or permanently – and as much a killer as it is a life-saver, people there generally depend upon the assistance and expertise of those who live or were trained in water-rich parts of the planet.

Water brings us together and pulls us apart. How we use it acts as a mirror, reflecting our societies and civilities back to ourselves. And, as I hope to show through this book, this is a good thing. Debates have become more vituperative over time, particularly over the 30-plus years of neoliberal globalisation. Left-wing social movements speak of water privatisation as a 'war against the poor'. Right-wing neo-realists speak of water as one more resource to be captured to ensure state power. Almost everyone invokes the 'water is finite' narrative as a motivator for action. My approach here is somewhat different. I begin from a position of a glass half full – in other words, that southern Africans are not 'running out of' water; rather, that there is enough water for all, forever, but it must be acknowledged that there are many serious problems related to water access, use, management and, in my view, above all, governance. Water is finite, but ever renewable, and while renewable it is fragile, for it can be altered by shifts in climate and in human practice. As will be demonstrated in subsequent chapters, the glass is also half full in the sense that, after more than two full decades of sustained water reforms within and among southern Africa's states, not a lot of progress has been made. What accounts for this situation is at the heart of this investigation.

As shown here, there is plenty of water in the world. Most of our most pressing water problems are human-made (so, admitting of amelioration through human intervention). Granted, there are water stresses all over the planet, but before we charge headlong into violent conflict, there are many pathways to co-operation. We are human: we have choice, but where choice requires change, change is never easy.

The boy who cried 'no wolf': Getting beyond alarmism

To attract people's attention we often resort to alarmism: 'Wars of the future will be about water!' said former head of the World Bank, Ismael Serageldin. And as much as 'the expert' abhors this statement, when given the opportunity to contribute to the UN document on new threats to security, we experts basically echoed Serageldin. How to justify 'crying wolf'? We felt there was no choice but to overstate the case to gain attention, and then try to work nuance into the argument from there. Has it worked? Not really. Those without ready access to potable water and adequate sanitation – numbering in the hundreds of millions – continue to struggle. Those with water and sanitation turn it to their political and economic advantage. That is a familiar story of poverty and inequality, only slightly less familiar as it relates to water resource access, use and management: a political economy of water, if you will. The whys and hows of that story as they relate to the southern African region will be told in the pages of this book.

Let us now briefly turn to a critical analysis of the current water alarmism.

Manufactured scarcity

Reproductions of the hydrological cycle often carry the heading 'Freshwater: finite and vulnerable', in line with Dublin Principle No. 1 (see Chapter 5). Schematic representations of all the water in the world, such as that put forward by organisations such as the Global Water Partnership, ask us to look at the resource available to us through a 'freshwater lens'. What we see there is that of the 100 per cent of all water on earth, an estimated 2.5 per cent is freshwater, of which only 0.3 per cent of that 2.5 per cent is readily accessible to humanity.

Aside from the facts that (1) a small percentage of a very large total is also a very large total; (2) this small percentage is *renewable*; and (3) technological innovations continue to make more freshwater available (more on this in subsequent chapters), there is little to be gained in dealing in aggregate figures. To characterise freshwater resources as scarce has less than zero social value; its negative value is that it prods those empowered and so inclined to capture the resource in the hopes of guaranteeing their own futures. We are witness to this in terms of 'land grabbing' across the African continent. As a 2012 study by University of the Western Cape (UWC) academic Barbara Tapela shows, what we really have is 'social water scarcity' – in other words, hundreds of millions of people at the margins of mainstream society lacking access to sufficient water for their needs due primarily to the indifference of empowered and well-watered social actors.

An important aspect of manufactured scarcity is the manipulation of perceptions regarding population. To wit: there is a finite sum of water on earth, but the human population keeps rising; how will we feed everyone? How will we find enough water for all? Organisations such as the World Resources Centre, the United Nations Development Programme and the World Bank foster this argument by juxtaposing increases in world water use with world population growth. This data shows exponential population growth and near exponential increases in global freshwater withdrawals, suggesting that the former directly causes the latter.

In a way, of course, this is true, especially in relation to rice production for domestic consumption in Asia. But it is also misleading and problematic. Given that water is in everything, and given that the vast majority of the world's resources are consumed in the global

North, it is more accurate to say that world consumption patterns drive world water use. As shown in the 2003 World Consumption Cartogram produced by Jerrad Pierce (see http://www.peopleandtheplanet.com/index.html@lid=26071&section=33&topic=26.html), Japan, Korea, most of the European Union (EU), especially Great Britain, and the United States account for the lion's share of global consumption. While China is increasing its global footprint, one must remember that a majority of the goods produced in China are exported for consumption elsewhere in the world.

Yet, to focus on population rather than consumption – or 'potential consumption' rather than 'actual consumption', as is often the case (i.e., the Western fear of middle-class India and China) – is to shift the focus of the world water crisis away from the global North to the countries of the global South, in particular India and now China, thereby absolving those who are the primary cause of a crisis of water over-consumption, consumers in America.

This is not to deny the very real problems created by urban growth in the global South, where huge concentrations of human populations create a host of very serious, but largely localised, problems. I deal with some of these issues in Chapter 4. What is being encouraged here, however, is a new way of seeing these issues and challenges. Over-simplified narratives built around 'scarcity' do little to move us forward to a world where there is some water for all forever.

We would do well to begin with the question, 'Where is the water, when, in what form, quality and quantity, and who has it deriving what benefits from it?' The natural follow-up question is, 'Why?' Most water experts agree that the primary unit of analysis should be the river basin. For scholars such as Malin Falkenmark and Johan Rockstrom (2004), while recognising that inter-basin transfer schemes are commonplace, starting from a position of where the water hits the soil – what Falkenmark and Rockstrom label 'green water' – is fundamental to a more nuanced approach to understanding and addressing 'water crises'.

State sovereignty and the fugitive nature of water

Transboundary waters are commonly understood as those shared by two or more states. As of 2009 there were an estimated 263 transboundary river basins, constituting 48 per cent of sovereign state territory, and 269 transboundary aquifers in the world. Within this setting there are about a dozen states with what Ken Conca (2006) describes as 'foreign water dependence' percentages over 80 per cent. According to former World Bank official David Grey:

> I would argue that in the 260 river basins across the planet that are shared by more than one state there are tensions in every single one of them, without exception, to a greater or lesser extent. In some cases it is so small you wouldn't see it and some cases very large indeed. So there is suspicion between all states that share river basins without exception, including in Africa.[1]

States, recognising no common power, arrogate to themselves the right to do whatever it is they wish with and to the resources within their own borders. For H.H.G. Savenije (2002), water is no ordinary good; it is fugitive and is often not found in the form, quantity or quality that we want it in, when or where we want it. (While India receives vast amounts of rainfall comparable to the UK, almost all of that water falls as monsoon rain over a few hundred hours every year.) These seemingly irreconcilable points of sovereign right to resources, shared basins, and the fugitive nature of water form the basis for the 'water wars' discourse. Nothing draws media and public attention like the spectre of war. Yet wars over water are surprisingly scarce.

In Peter Gleick's (2000a) 'chronology of water conflict', which non-systematically covered a period of 500 years, water was seen to be a political or military tool, a military target, an object of terrorism, part of a development dispute, or an object of control. Most of his

---

1. http://www.irinnews.org/printreport.aspx?reportid=46125.

cases involved inter-state activity, although intra-state conflicts were sometimes reported. In no case was water the principal cause of two states going to war. Given that 145 states and 40 per cent of the global population falls within 263 international river basins that account for 60 per cent of global river flow, this is not an insignificant finding: the opportunities for violent conflict are abundant, yet such instances are extremely rare. According to Aaron Wolf and his colleagues (2005: 84), '[N]o states have gone to war specifically over water resources since the city-states of Lagash and Umma fought each other in the Tigris-Euphrates basin in 2500 BC. Instead, according to the UN Food and Agriculture Organisation, more than 3 600 water treaties were signed from AD 805 to 1984.'

In two empirical studies, Nils Petter Gleditsch and colleagues examined probabilities of violent conflict between two states sharing a river (Toset, Gleditsch and Hegre 2000), and among states sharing the waters of a river basin (Gleditsch et al. 2006). In the former, the threshold for violent conflict was one fatality; in the latter, the threshold was 25 fatalities taken from the Correlates of War Project database. The researchers found that 'while the frequency of Militarized Interstate Dispute outbreaks in the dyads with no risk factors is 0.3 per cent, it increases to 10 per cent in dyads with shared rivers, no democracies, two great powers, low economic development in both countries, for the post-World War II time period' (Toset, Gleditsch and Hegre 2000). In the basin-wide study in 2006, Gleditsch and fellow authors showed that 'peace history' was the greatest predictor of co-operation among states with shared borders. At the same time, areas prone to violent conflict showed one or more of the following characteristics: unconsolidated regimes, single democracy, two autocracies, major power (strong predictors); dyad size, shared basin, and percentage upstream (moderate predictors); development, length of boundary, basin size, basin upstream, and number of river crossings (weak predictors). The authors conclude, 'Our new dataset reinforces the conclusion from the earlier studies that there is some relationship between shared river basins and conflict . . . [T]his article refers mainly to low-level conflict and our results are not to be taken as evidence of impending "water wars". Low-level interstate conflict in no way excludes cooperation; indeed it may be an important incentive for more cooperation. The three-way relationship (shared rivers-conflict-cooperation) also remains to be investigated' (Gleditsch et al. 2006: 380).

In a summary of work conducted at Oregon State University in 2005, Wolf and his team highlight four key findings: first, 'the incidence of acute conflict over international water resources is overwhelmed by the rate of cooperation'; second, 'despite the fiery rhetoric of politicians ... most actions taken over water are mild'; third, 'there are more examples of cooperation than of conflict'; and fourth, 'despite the lack of violence, water acts as both an irritant and a unifier'. In conclusion, the authors state, 'The historical record proves that international water disputes do get resolved, even among enemies, and even as conflicts erupt over other issues. Some of the world's most vociferous enemies have negotiated water agreements or are in the process of doing so, and the institutions they have created often prove to be resilient, even when relations are strained' (2005: 85). The authors put great stock in institutional capacity, arguing that it is the key to co-operation in situations of increasing scarcity. Tony Allan (2002, 2003) has argued that water has not been an object of conflict in the Middle East partly because the region's chronic water deficit is compensated for through the importation of food – in essence, the region imports 'virtual water' contained in the manufacture of foodstuffs, allowing people in Middle Eastern countries to enjoy a standard of living beyond their natural water barriers. So, there may be many other factors at play in either the onset or the absence of inter-state violent conflict.

Gleditsch and colleagues have been at the forefront of this analysis, most recently as related to climate change and armed conflict (see Buhaug, Gleditsch and Theisen 2010; Nordås and Gleditsch 2007; Gleditsch 2012). The Stockholm International Water Institute (SIWI) has also attempted to link global water crises to both the post-Millennium Development Goals (MDGs) and climate change and security discourses. According to the World Economic Forum (2011), most recently water has been linked to energy, food and climate in a 'security nexus'. At the heart of all of these lies the alarmist position that water is scarce, finite and threatened, that population growth leads us beyond planetary carrying capacities, and that sovereign states may be forced to take matters into their own hands when it comes to the water, food, energy security nexus. The evidence that links violent inter-state conflict directly to water is, however, simply not there.

The real 'water war'

Vandana Shiva (2002) and others have written about a different sort of 'water war': a war waged by the rich upon the poor – through what they see as the reckless and deliberate capture of land and water resources for commercial agricultural purposes; through the pollution and/or draining of local aquifers by multinational mining companies; through the privatisation of urban water services delivery systems that deepen access by the rich while ignoring the poor; by the decimation of forests; and, lately, through land grabbing. This is tantamount to a water-wars counter-narrative centred on what Lyla Mehta (2001, 2007) labelled 'socially constructed water scarcity' that regards the state, in league with private corporations, as often antagonistic toward its own citizens. The dynamics leading to these outcomes are only recently being taken up by scholars such as Bernauer and Böhmelt (2012) working in the water and conflict mainstream.

While there are numerous advocates for affordable urban water for all, they have tended to align inequitable access in urban areas with the alarmist discourse of a crisis of scarcity. Savenije (2002), as well as Falkenmark and Rockstrom (2004), equate this to a 'blue water bias', mistakenly identifying what are essentially politically driven urban failures as a key feature of wider system stresses (primarily brought about by damming, diverting and draining).

The 'hard cases'

In my view, the sovereign state, as the universally accepted purveyor of bounded law and order, stands at the centre of all water questions, conundrums and challenges. Crises within the state have been characterised as a consequence of poor and weak governance and have been disciplined through a management narrative involving building state capacity, letting the private sector lead in urban provision, and non-governmental organisations (NGOs) lead in rural water delivery. Analysis rarely goes beyond the need for improved systems, policies, laws and procedures. Where these fail, the explanation is invariably attributed to a lack of political will. The superficiality of this literature can be attributed to its liberal theoretical take on 'the state' and the 'system of states', where all states are considered equal in law but unequal in capacities. Missing are the structural characteristics of an unequal global political economy, wherein the state may be regarded as a highly contested social form dominated by different coalitions of actors over time.

Analyses of inter-state competition overwhelmingly focus on what Mark Zeitoun and Jeroen Warner (2006) label 'hydro-hegemony' – in other words, the notion that within transboundary river basins there is usually a disparity of power between sovereign state actors leading to uneven outcomes in resource sharing and often persistent, generally low-level disputes between riparian parties. The literature returns again and again to the 'hard cases', i.e., the Nile, Indus, Ganges and Brahmaputra, Mekong, Tigris-Euphrates and Jordan river basins: all located in highly populated areas, with hard states, more-or-less authoritarian governments and weak civil societies whose politicians tend to play at realist geopolitics. This may be contrasted with the basin states of much of sub-Saharan Africa that are, in Larry Bowman's (1968) memorable term, penetrated-political-economic systems, with porous borders, and highly mobile and integrated civil societies and social networks. The contrasting nature of these states and civil societies, as well as the contrasting antagonistic versus co-operative regional inter-state dynamics makes for very different outcomes in transboundary water governance and management. Yet the co-operative cases gain little traction as fears of resource wars in an age of climate change gain both attention and research funding.

Toward a different story

In this book I aim to tell a different story while using the same data and drawing from the same sources as my mainstream colleagues. While focusing on the same set of important issues, my point of departure is that meaningful change requires co-ordinated struggle not compliance and new public management. In part, continuing difficulties around fairer and more sustainable forms of water use emanate from a fatalist discourse attached to common constructs, systems and conceptualisations of water. As a result, the world as it is today appears to be on a linear path toward disaster: failed states, bankrupt municipalities, too many mouths to feed, not enough water for cities and farms – with most of these issues located in the global South. Part of the problem is that the conceptual and physical tools we depend on to 'solve' our problems are the same ones that brought us to this point in the first place.

We must see water differently. We must see the state and other social forms differently. We must ask unconventional questions. We must invent the world we want in light of the world we have before us; we must bring agency to bear upon structure. How can we do this? Fortunately, we are not alone in either our thinking or our desire. There are pockets of creativity all around. Let us begin with a few examples.

Africa and the 'hydraulic mission'

If we examine the data for average rainfall per annum across the African continent, what it shows us is a very dry north, east and southwest of the continent; an extremely wet middle; and a relatively well-watered band in between these two extremes. If we compare this data with figures for populations with limited access to safe drinking water and improved sanitation, we see that a large percentage of this group is to be found in the wettest parts of the continent. At the same time, available data shows these 'wet' states to have small water footprints. According to the International Water Management Institute, what this tells us is that it is not physical water scarcity that plagues much of the African continent, particularly the most heavily populated parts, but *economic water scarcity* defined as a situation where less than 25 per cent of available blue water flow is harnessed for development purposes due to a variety of human, institutional and financial constraints.

Most of Africa's water-related development challenges stem from what Tony Allan (2003) defines as an incomplete hydraulic mission, i.e., capturing available water resources for human and socio-economic development. This insight helps move us away from the common perception that Africa lacks sufficient water for developmental purposes.

Among the many values of Allan's articulation of the hydraulic mission over time is the way it helps us see not only increasing world water use, particularly in the post-1950, 'high modern' era, but that there continues to be a contentious discourse between high-consumption countries (primarily those comprising the Organisation for Economic Co-operation and Development, OECD) and low-consumption countries, especially China and India whose ambitions to become 'like the West' in terms of their development and consumption profiles is undeniable. Allan shows that over the last few decades, different discourses or paradigms have emerged on the back of new knowledge to frame discussions on the best ways and means to use water for human purposes. Environmental, economic and political framings have emerged to expose the fallacies that the world of water is simply there for the taking, available to satisfy the whim and whimsy of every engineer, industrialist and politician around the world. These new perspectives have had a positive impact on OECD consumption practices: economies continue to grow while using considerably less water. But world water use continues to rise as China and India pursue their own late-modern hydraulic missions. As will be shown here, Africa too is interested in this developmental pathway, with Ethiopia's pursuit of the Grand Renaissance Dam being the most recent example. This book focuses on the states of the Southern African Development Community (SADC), currently comprising fifteen states in the region: Angola, Botswana, Democratic Republic of the Congo, Lesotho, Madagascar, Malawi, Mauritius, Mozambique, Namibia, Seychelles, South Africa, Swaziland, Tanzania, Zambia and Zimbabwe.

Emphasis is placed on the twelve member states located on the mainland of the subcontinent. This is because the island member states share no transboundary water and face quite a different set of challenges unique to small island developing states (SIDS). The organisation was created in 1992 to accommodate a newly majority-ruled South Africa. Prior to 1992, the SADC was called the Southern African Development Co-ordination Conference (SADCC), itself formed in 1980. SADC states have a well-articulated infrastructure development plan (see Chapter 5), which looks suspiciously like 1950s-style development across the global North. If anything unites states and civil societies across the southern African region, it is the desire to harness the region's water for human use. In these pages, the character of this hydraulic mission will be examined.

Feeding the continent one farmer's fields at a time

A second example follows from the insights above. In their 2004 study, Falkenmark and Rockstrom argue that food security policy must begin with an understanding of the hydrological cycle and place its emphasis on where the raindrop hits the soil. Their aim is to achieve 'water for humans and nature' as well as 'more crop per drop'. In their view, we must see water in its various colours, especially green water, if we are to devise adequate approaches to food security and/or food sovereignty. Even in very dry regions, there is generally enough rainfall – if well managed – to successfully and regularly produce food crops. Rather than obsess over blue water withdrawals through irrigation technology, we would do well to focus on rainfall with the aim of shifting water-vapour flows from evaporation to transpiration through food crops. Seeing water in its many colours helps us see that there is often more water and therefore more policy choices available to us than we hitherto believed.

Toward better food policy through an understanding of virtual water

Simply put, virtual water is the amount of water used in the production of a commodity. It is most commonly applied to foodstuffs. Central and

Northern Africa are heavy exporters of virtual water. This is because, in the words of Ali Mazrui (1986), African economies are 'beverage economies' – growing and exporting the raw materials that go into many of the world's favoured beverages: sugar, coffee, tea, cocoa, fruits and vegetables of all kinds. In addition to other commercial agricultural crops such as tobacco, maize and cotton, most of these commodities are shipped out raw or only minimally beneficiated. Many South American and Central/South Asian economies find themselves in the same bind, some actually being net importers of virtual water through the export of cotton in exchange for foodstuffs. Allan (2002) highlights how such virtual water trade allows the Middle East to live 'beyond the natural water barrier'. And whereas both Canada and the United States are heavy exporters of virtual water, they face very different problems created by their crop production practices: e.g., from declining aquifers in the Central/Southwestern United States to an unhealthy and possibly unsustainable dependence on glacial melt runoff to grow alfalfa for cattle in Canada's otherwise bone-dry southern Alberta.

Like 'green water', 'virtual water' is a concept that helps us see water differently. It helps us understand what we are doing with the water resources we have and to ask tough questions regarding whether these are good choices. Shifting agricultural practices is a difficult political game, so never easy. But if we are to make the best use of the water we have for the citizens who most need it, we need the proper tools to help widen the decision-making landscape as much as possible.

Water in development

Ken Conca describes our approach to the use of water in development as 'pushing rivers around'. In his insightful 2006 study of the use of water in development, he divides chapter headings under damming, diverting and draining. In terms of 'damming', we have managed to create an estimated 800 000 dams, of which there are about 40 000 whose main wall is greater than 15 metres in height. With regard to 'diverting', more than one half of all large dams are created with large-scale irrigation in mind. Conca points out that between 30 and 40 per cent of the world's

271 million hectares of irrigated land is 'dam dependent'. Lastly, in term of 'draining', the vast majority of the world's wetlands have been drained, with 80 per cent of what remains being 'threatened'. Tony Allan (2003) highlights how much of this activity occurred over a 100-year period (roughly 1880–1980) of 'industrial modernity' where humans unreflectively believed that nature could be mastered. South African scholars Bryan Davies and Jenny Day, in their important 1998 study entitled *Vanishing Waters*, provide a detailed and trenchant accounting of the effects of the hydraulic mission in southern Africa.

While the hydraulic mission has successfully delivered development benefits to large swaths of the global population, it has also wreaked havoc on local ecologies and displaced and/or marginalised millions of people. The worst ecological consequences of the hydraulic mission can be seen across the countries comprising the former Soviet Union, with the decimation of the Aral Sea in the name of cotton production being perhaps the best example. But there are many such cases. In 2009 Meena Palaniappan and Peter Gleick wrote about 'peak ecological water', meaning that beyond a certain ratio of renewal to withdrawal, a local ecology reaches a tipping point at which it changes fundamentally and permanently to something else. Lake Chad may be one such case, as incessant withdrawals have reduced the lake to a fraction of the size it was at the time of African state independence in the 1960s, turning what was once one of Africa's premier inland seas into a rather shallow lake surrounded by grassland.

In his 2003 study, Allan highlights how, in the Western world, developmental processes have taken on the reflective insights of environmental scholarship, as well as the cost-benefit analysis of economics. However, in the southern African region, the 2012 SADC Infrastructure Division's development master plan looks very much like old style development: big dams, more canals, for mines and cash-crop plantations. Given the penetration of norms and ideas along with capital and technical assistance from global North to global South, will these new ways of seeing water trickle down into the region?

Or must we commit the sins of the past? Have we learned nothing? Is there not a different path to development that can be environmentally sustainable, economically efficient and socially equitable (the so-called 'Triple-E bottom line' of Integrated Water Resources Management, IWRM)? If we cannot revolutionise our practices, can we not at least learn from our mistakes, and make significant reforms? These are some of the key questions being asked by the world's water experts today. They have gained a coherent shape around IWRM – a dominant but contested framework for thinking about alternative forms of development centred on social, ecological and economic sustainability. IWRM has been discussed and debated globally by scholars such as Pieter van der Zaag (2005), Douglas Merrey (2008) and Asit Biswas (2008) and in the region by people such as Lewis Jonker (2008) and Emmanuel Manzungu (e.g., Manzungu and Derman, 2016; Movik, Mehta and Manzungu, 2016).

In search of IWRM

The needs and pressures for an IWRM approach are clear. Burgeoning mega-cities have created massive pressures on existing infrastructures and resource bases. Women continue to find themselves at the lowest end of the technological water resource chain, being responsible for water in the household but largely marginalised from commercial or large-scale systems of delivery. Climate change is altering hydrological regimes, with many glacial-melt-dependent social systems being threatened due to the dynamics of warmer climates (e.g., decreased snow pack, earlier and longer melt periods, glacial lake outburst flooding). Inter-state development dynamics drive resource use mimicry despite widely differing hydrological cycles, with Muammar Gaddafi's attempt to 'green the Libyan desert' being one such scheme. According to the UNDP, the twentieth century saw a sixfold increase in freshwater withdrawals. Without doubt, we face many new and more serious pressures on our systems. More of the same sorts of practices (as we are seeing in places as diverse as Brazil, China, India and Mali) will only make matters worse. We must see water differently, so we can see the opportunities among the many challenges.

Five points to ponder

As I close this introductory chapter, let me leave you with five points to ponder, after which I briefly explain the contents of the book.

First, *our problems are human-made* and, make no mistake, they are many. But as they are human made, we can unmake many of them. We have a choice in where and how we live, in what we consume and in what quantities, in how we produce our goods and services. Since water is in everything, these are not water-specific issues; they are much more broadly public policy issues, touching on our notions of shared social projects, and of the good society.

Second, we *mustn't mistake urban water issues for issues of water scarcity*. Urban water, in the words of Tony Allan (2003), is 'small water'. The amount of water we need for our daily personal needs in the household and in the community, even extending to economic water for small business operations, is but a tiny fraction of the water used in agriculture. Whereas people require anywhere between 18 to 108 m^3/person/year – in other words, between 50 and 300 litres/person/day – for personal consumption, we need anywhere between 600 to 1800 m^3/person/year in water for food. This does not mean that small water issues are themselves small issues; they are central to the quality of life of the individual and the character of a society. Where people lack access to potable water and/or water-borne sanitation, this is not a scarcity issue, it is a political issue. Decision-makers have all the water they require; they sit far from the squatter settlement or rural backwater; their allies are industrialists and commercial farmers whose water needs must be met if the politician is to retain his or her power. The so-called 'urban water war' in Cochabamba, Bolivia, is a reminder of the power of the dispossessed and the marginalised. Politicians would do well to reflect on this fact.

Third, we *have choice in how and where we grow food and other commercial crops*. As articulated in the second World Water Development Report, globally, 'rain-fed farming represents 82 per cent of cropland and the bulk of the world's agricultural production' (WWDR II 2006). Yields expressed as metric tonnes/hectare (t/ha) vary greatly across rain-fed farming zones. In general, yields are greater in temperate zones (7–10 t/ha) where water is more reliable, soils more fertile and resilient, and evaporative demand much lower, as opposed to humid, semi-humid, semi-arid and arid zones (often <1 t/ha) where soils are more fragile, drought and/or flood common occurrences, and rainfall regimes more erratic, intense and patchy. Yet these savanna zones constitute the primary areas of rain-fed subsistence agriculture and water-dependent pastoralism practised across sub-Saharan Africa and South Asia. For Falkenmark and Rockstrom (2004), huge gains in food production may be made through 'vapour shift' – in other words, ensuring that green water passes through the root zones of food crops rather than evaporating straight back to the atmosphere from atop parched soils, hardpan, and so on. These are partly management issues (see Chapter 4), but they are also overwhelmingly questions of social justice within fragile and weak state forms. Global agreements, such as the Paris Agreement on climate, put pressure on southern African states to cut carbon emissions. Several are turning to biofuel production as a means of meeting their COP21 commitments, and generating income to service national debt and finance services and subsidise foodstuffs in urban areas. So, as rural farmers need assistance in achieving 'more crop per drop', instead many are becoming tenant farmers on vast plantations watered by means of expensive and elaborate irrigation systems that feed no one. This is not an inevitable outcome, with the lessons of Cochabamba being relevant here.

Deliberate decisions have been taken in every case to create, nurture and maintain the systems of agricultural production, distribution and consumption. Rather than opine the scarcity of the world's water, it seems to me to be time for a broad conversation about consumption, and about the winners and losers along the global food chain. This is particularly so as many states see fresh revenue streams in increased biofuel production.

Fourth, *rather than worry about inter-state violent conflicts around water, we should recognise, celebrate and build upon the facts that everywhere we make agreements and solve disputes.* As highlighted above, there is a long history of co-operation on shared resources. This is especially so at the local level. As stated previously, water is not an ordinary good: among other things, it is bulky and non-substitutable, so people generally reside where they use the resource. While water use may cause many local conflicts, these are generally resolved because the resource is non-substitutable. This is not to say that co-operation always equals fair outcomes, or that forms of negotiation foster improved social capital. There are many cases of stable patterns of local water use where the majority flows toward society's most powerful actors, while barely a trickle flows to the poor. (If there is one lesson to be learned from the hydraulic mission, it is that water does not always flow along the hydraulic gradient; most often it flows toward money.)

Also, sometimes the geography of immediate, local need stands in stark contrast to the power of distant political and economic capital. Put differently, sometimes water resembles oil, with the benefits to be derived from its direct or associated use outweighing the cost and complexity of the system of delivery. The poster-child for such a project, of course, is the Colorado River. But there are many other examples, where, for example, local Native American freshwater springs now run dry because electricity companies have drained the underlying aquifer sluicing raw coal across the length of Nevada to be burned for electricity to service the state of California. Many environmentalists are currently sounding the alarm around fracking, while in Canada the oil sands project is having significant local impacts on the Athabasca River system.

Thus, my point here is that we should not be complacent because historical records suggest co-operation; rather, we should look carefully at these instances of co-operation, recognise the often uneven benefits derived from sharing agreements in order to derive new understandings that foster wider co-operation and more inclusive benefit generation.

Fifth and finally, we should *recognise that the real water war is that being waged against the poor*. The rich always have water, generally more than they will ever need, or even imagine needing. Water is in everything; its condition mirrors the world. Thus, the so-called 'champagne glass of global income inequality', first described by the UNDP in 1992, wherein the top 20 per cent control 80 per cent of the income, is really a water glass. Another way of viewing the world consumption cartogram is to see states such as the US as bloated with water, while whole continents such as South America and Africa are drained nearly dry. Liberal reformism is unlikely to achieve its hoped-for goals; while it is my personal feeling that more radical approaches will be necessary if we are to ensure some water for all forever, it is also my strong belief that we can achieve significant change segmentally, i.e., whenever and wherever possible. While IWRM presents us with an overarching framework, we should proceed when and wherever we can.

The book

This book is not intended to be the final word on water resources governance and management in southern Africa. To the contrary, there is a massive literature out there, much of it highlighted in the selected bibliography. Rather, my aim is to put forward a structured argument regarding why the glass remains half full – neither filling nor tipping out the rest of its contents. The region appears to be in stasis, with hopeful signs but persistent and disappointing trends. My argument is that the structure of the region's political economy creates a paradoxical situation where sustainable and equitable water use cannot happen unless southern African states move off the extractive industry/cash-crop commodity track; however, the rewards reaped by those at the centre of power are such that there is little incentive to change. At the same time, neoliberal globalisation encourages more of the same. Indeed, there is a positive spin to this continuing resource dependence in the form of the 'Africa rising' narrative. So what you will see here is a wide array of pluses and minuses. My recommendation is to not lose sight of the fact that while things may look bleak from the lofty and insulated position of the ivory tower, people on the ground do not have time for pessimism. They need water for their daily livelihoods and they need it now. During my long tenure in the region, this was always my approach, which leads to an action agenda that is, in Canadian scholar Robert Cox's (1996) words, organised around clinical – not cynical –

political action. As shown in Chapter 4, there is a great deal of clinical politics being practised in cities around the region.

In support of this argument, the book proceeds as follows: Chapter 2 locates the present water resources problematic in the context of a history of colonial and imperial underdevelopment; Chapter 3 explores the region's water resources, while Chapter 4 examines how it is used, with an emphasis on use patterns at national level and domestic water supply in urban and rural areas; Chapter 5 switches to the international arena and describes the various ways and means of transboundary water use in the region. Chapter 6 provides a summary and reflections on a hopeful way forward.

2

Mapping Underdevelopment

Toward a Political Economy of Water in Southern Africa

In the beginning there was nature, and where there were people they were part of nature, part of the landscape, part of the natural rhythms of synergistic systems comprising the animate and inanimate, the sentient and non-sentient, the short-lived and the near-eternal. How things have changed. The so-called 'first peoples of the Kalahari' were, in fact, first peoples of southern Africa, whose domain extended almost throughout the region. Cornelis Vanderpost, in a 2000 study of 'naming', illustrated that Khoisan habitation was extensive, and to claim that they were absent or that the lands were empty, as the colonists did, was done either out of ignorance or with the intention of dispossessing those first peoples, ultimately banishing them to the sands of the Kalahari. Hunter-gatherers followed the animals and the seasonal fecundity of the land. Ultimately, they were following water resources, specifically the rains, whose presence or absence in the interior was primarily a function of the transit of the sun across the Inter-Tropical Convergence Zone and between the tropics of Capricorn and Cancer. So, to those places of absence the bushmen would again and again return and, in the process, give them names. Over a period of centuries, however, the Khoisan were displaced by successive waves of migrants: Bantu-speaking peoples between 2 500 and 1 000 years ago, and thereafter Europeans as imperialists, colonists and settlers. Initially, according to the renowned Cambridge professor of History, John Illiffe (1995), the struggle was over processes of production, with shifting agriculture and pastoralism winning out over hunter-gatherer societies. While all these societies were more or less mobile, those who had domesticated crops and animals were better able to generate a surplus, and so devise the divisions of labour and the developments of culture that gave rise to the great kingdoms of Africa. The nomads' only choice was to inhabit the margins, to eke out an existence in spaces of least interest to cattle keepers and maize growers.

Unlike the kingdoms and empires of Europe, African rulers were less concerned with the creation of physical borders – in other words, determining 'what's mine' on the land through a line in the sand – than they were with secure relations among neighbouring peoples (i.e., determining 'who are mine' through allegiance and alliance). To paraphrase American scholar Jeffrey Herbst (2000): in Europe people were many, but land was scarce and so valuable; in Africa, it was the other way around, people were most valued. African cosmologies, and therefore cultures and political economies, were very different from European ones, so the comparison of 'value' is somewhat off the mark. But the primary point holds: the European resource fetish, initially the insatiable demand for slaves and other tradable commodities, such as gemstones and ivory, and latterly in its nineteenth-century full-blown imperial 'scramble for Africa', resulted in a fundamental break of a majority of African people's relationships with the landscape, nature and each other; everywhere it led to a distortion of the cultures and social forms founded on the rhythm and mobility of seasonality.

In my considered opinion, the colonial period – brief though it was – has had a profound and lasting impact on Africa. The formal period marked the apex of a centuries-long engagement with the continent, the ultimate effect being to take self-defining societies and transform them into social forms whose *raison d'être* was to service the needs of the mercantile empires and later emergent and antagonistic capitalist states of Europe. Put simply, Africa was turned inside out. Granted, as Fanon and Wallerstein and many others have argued, there were many local beneficiaries in this process. But one wonders about choice. To paraphrase Zimbabwean professor Solomon Nkiwane (1988), first the

Europeans took away our gods, then they took away our land; and they were able to do so because they were armed with the great god 'Gun'.

At first glance, the relevance of African history to present-day water resource management may not be clear. The colonialists have long departed; new technological innovations are regularly rolled out across the region; independent states have created legal and institutional frameworks for the access and use of water; many have up-to-date water resource strategies, laws and policies. Yet many problems persist and new challenges emerge almost as quickly as old ones are successfully addressed. Why is this so? In the water sector, the answer is most often either that 'there is a lack of (human, financial, technical) capacity' or that 'there is a lack of political will'. Neither of these answers, however, gets to the nub of the issue. In my view, if we are to move toward better forms and practices of water governance and management, we must acknowledge the depth and extent of the socio-economic and socio-political pathologies that give rise to present poor practice. Only in this way will we begin to be able to devise water resources access, use and management strategies and practices to the benefit of all – in other words, achieve 'some water for all for ever', in the words of South Africa's Department of Water Affairs (DWA). I now turn to a discussion of the most salient of these factors.

The state

With the creation of formal borders delimiting the extent of competing claims by imperial powers in Africa, the 1884 Berlin Conference set the stage for the 'extraversion' of African political economies. No longer were Africans the masters of their own destinies; under colonial rule Africa was reorganised to satisfy the needs, tastes and whims of Europeans. In the late 1980s, Ali Mazrui (1986) rightly characterised Africa's states as 'beverage economies'. Almost 30 years later, little has changed. Along with beverage crops – e.g., sugar, tea, coffee, cocoa, fruits of all kinds – many African states have been organised around cash crops such as wheat, rice, tobacco, and the extraction of oil, minerals and gemstones. The long histories of intra-African production and trade, and African-defined trade with the near and far East, have been overturned almost completely. Anyone who has taken public transit across Africa knows how widely the theory of regional integration diverges from the reality of queues, delays, searches, fines and bribes at the borders between states. While three decades of structural adjustment conditionalities ensured the non-diversification of African economies away from these raw materials, these patterns have been presently augmented by a new scramble for African resources. This new stage of resource dependency is driven by the rise of China as the second largest economy in the world, and by the widespread discovery of oil and gas across the continent

There is a common joke made about the copperbelt in Zambia. It goes something like this: a plane flies over central Africa. Two people are looking out the window. 'What is that giant hole down there?' asks one of the passengers. 'That used to be Zambia,' says the other. More ironic than funny, it seems to me, as the world races to empty the continent of its wealth. From the standpoint of sustainability, Africa's states are anything but. Yet the people who run these 'lame leviathans', to quote Tom Callaghy (1987), readily participate in the rape and pillage of the continent.

Scrambling for Africa is a thirsty game, and the vast majority of the region's water resources have been captured to slake this thirst. Africa is a net exporter of its water resources. This is another way of illustrating the long-valuable observation about uneven terms of trade: Africa exports raw materials (i.e., goods that are heavily dependent on water resources use such as beverage crops and precious metals) and imports finished goods (which are more water efficient).

Sovereignty and its tropes virtually ensure that Africa's political leaders will seek solutions to unsustainability through the same channels that gave rise to it in the first place. Borders have divided a continent whose natural rhythms run counter to the arrow-straight lines drawn across deserts and forests; or at the bank of a river; or in the middle of a stream flow; or in the valley between two mountains. At independence, Africa's leaders accepted Kwame Nkrumah's dictum to 'seek ye first the political kingdom, and all else shall follow unto you'. At the time, perhaps, this seemed sensible: gain political power – autonomy – and sort out the rest later. While recognising that hindsight is 20/20, evidence shows that this has proven to be the road to permanent instability. Even where states are 'stable', there are chronic pathologies such as permanent underclasses, widespread resource degradation and emerging tensions, such as rates of urban population growth, that far outstrip municipal capacity to deliver essential services.

Fortunately, like people everywhere, Africans are not content to reside in their 'state box'. Intra-African parallel economies in goods and services have sprung up in response to hitherto unmet needs, so recreating some of the mobility and rhythm natural to the region. Of course, avoiding the state or leaving the state to operate as a conduit for the region's resources out of the continent assists neither in strengthening state-civil society relations, nor in reshaping African political economies to meet the needs of present and future generations of the states' citizens. Yet the fact that smallholder farmers band together to co-operatively grow cabbages for a local albeit 'transnational' market suggests to me reasons for optimism. I am not ignoring the fact that African elites are at the same time negotiating, on behalf of the state (and by extension, for the common good), land grabs so that rice can be produced by Asians for Asians. They have served as *compradors nonpareil*. But we have to start somewhere. Besides, these are not mutually exclusive processes. Both point to the pathologies of the African state form, a state form in need of radical reconstruction if the African resource base is not to be irreparably plundered for the good of the few in the continent and beyond.

Modes of production

If the colonial state form legitimated resource exploitation for extra-African ends, then the system of road, rail and sea transportation developed during this era facilitated its realisation. In examining a map of the railroad infrastructure developed across the southern African region, three things are immediately apparent. First, South Africa's rail system is by far the most extensively developed, linking together most parts of the country. Second, much the rest of the region's railroads are linked into South Africa's system. Only the Tazara (Tanzania-Zambia Railway) rail line, and the Beira Corridor line (linking Zimbabwe to the sea through the Mozambican port of Beira) interlink independent southern African states with each other. Each of these lines was the consequence of the regional struggle for national independence and freedom from apartheid South Africa's regional domination. Third, there is a patchwork of rail lines that extends from the coast to the interior, seemingly stopping in the middle of nowhere, but in fact beginning at mine heads.

Whereas Africa's rivers were its pre-colonial, life-giving arteries that pulsed with trade, transportation and settlement, the colonial era turned these into convenient boundaries, constricting their flow and rerouting the region's lifeblood – its people, its resources – to clot densely around mine heads and plantations, before flowing out through the rail lines to the sea and then on to Europe. Moreover, the rivers themselves were dammed and diverted and the wetlands drained, in service of these new modes and relations of production.

It is something of a paradox that the region's most industrially developed state, South Africa, is also one of its least well endowed in terms of those water resources necessary to drive industry, mining and agribusiness. First under colonial and later under independent (pre- and apartheid) rule, South Africa reached across its own borders to capture the land, labour and capital necessary for regional dominance and ultimately continental economic pre-eminence. Migrant labour flowed into the mines and onto the farms, as electricity flowed from the turbines at Cahora Bassa to power South African industry. At the same time, this latticework of regional power grids and transportation infrastructure was complemented with an increasingly complex network of water delivery infrastructure, as South Africa engaged in its own hydraulic mission.

While Paul Collier and Anke Hoeffler (1998, 2002, 2004) at the World Bank have talked about the 'resource curse' in Africa, suggesting among other things that over-reliance on one or a small group of primary commodity exports leads to socio-political instability and violent conflict, one might make the more accurate observation that the entire structure of southern Africa reflects what Thomas Homer-Dixon (1994) described as resource capture and ecological marginalisation, with highly unstable political economies (such as the Democratic Republic of Congo, DRC) at one extreme, and relatively more stable political economies (such as Botswana and Malawi) at the other extreme. Rather than violent conflict, this resource capture has led almost everywhere to what Johan Galtung (1971) defined as 'structural violence'. In Homer-Dixon's analysis, this form of violence is 'sub-national, persistent and diffuse'.

In my view, few graphics illustrate the region's challenges better than the rail system. The rail system is a visual proxy for a combination of more academic and technical explanations: dual economies; rentier states dependent upon extractive industries; enclave development; uneven terms of trade; formal and informal sectors; shadow states; poor governance and weak civil societies. Most of the facts derived through these conceptual frameworks stand at odds with the 'emerging Africa' narrative now dominant in the international financial institutions and state houses of the global North. How can one be so optimistic about 'emergence' when simply more of the same suggests a continued narrow insertion into a painfully unequal and highly unstable capitalist world economic system?

Water is embedded in the production and distribution of all goods and services. As such, the region's freshwater resources have been commandeered to serve the mines, plantations, large commercial agricultural enterprises, industries and select neighbourhoods of the cities. Just as the Ethiopian scholar Fantu Cheru (1997) speaks of 'global apartheid', one can also speak of 'water apartheid', because the vast majority of the region's peasant farmers depend on rainfall over small plots, as opposed to the complex irrigated systems stretching from large dams to the prime lands 'owned' by local and global multinational corporate capital. Similarly, the well-watered suburbs of Windhoek, Luanda, Lusaka, Harare, Maputo, Johannesburg and Cape Town (each located in a very different sort of micro-climate with a highly specific hydrological cycle) stand side by side with the densely packed townships and squatter settlements served predominantly by occasionally functioning standpipes delivering water of variable quality.

Human settlement

In perusing a map of human settlement patterns in southern Africa, five trends are readily discernible, three of which correspond closely with the rail map. First, among regional states, South Africa alone departs from the common Third World model of one primate city, followed by a number of significantly less populated urban centres: industrial deepening being reflected in the number and variety of urban forms. Second, the region shows a predominance of coastal settlement coupled with large inland agglomerations clustered primarily, but not only, around extractive processes. Inland and coastal settlements are connected by rail lines designed to aggregate the resources being extracted (e.g., minerals) or grown (e.g., tobacco, tea) for transshipment to the coast for export. In most cases, all roads lead to South Africa. Third, the region is dotted with small mining towns or regional centres, their locations determined by the development of a mine (e.g., Selebi Phikwe) or a cluster of farms (e.g., Mutare). The most dramatic instance of this is Kimberley, in South Africa. In some ways, it is a typical mining town whose fortunes have waned since diamonds were discovered there in the 1860s. Now a tourist site, the Big Hole from which these first diamonds were mined – manually, I might add – is in fact the epicentre of the region's history. Despite its considerable size (surface area of 17 hectares, 463 metres wide, 240 metres deep), only one hand-car brimming full of diamonds was ever mined from this place, but that hand-car full of diamonds financed the subsequent gold-mining boom on the reef, which ultimately led to the South African (Anglo-Boer) War (1899–1902), state independence (1910), regional patterns of trade and migration with South Africa as the hub and, as stated earlier, continental economic pre-eminence. All because of a hole in the ground at the edge of the Karoo.

The other two trends reflect either anomaly or history. With regard to anomaly, several very large settlements reflect the transformation of small settlements initially established because of proximity to a water resource (e.g., Windhoek), or strategic location (e.g., Maseru, Bulawayo). With time, these became sites of permanent settlement under colonial administration. With regard to history, Africa's persistent dual economic structure (i.e., peasant agriculture alongside agribusiness, and formal economies born of extractive industries alongside informal economies born of petty commodity trade) means that some historical patterns of production, settlement and reproduction were never completely displaced by colonialism/imperialism. Those regional states clustered around the African Great Lakes show numerous settlements reflective of intra-African production and trade. They for the most part stood beyond the reach of imperial need (though today, what was once remote and thought to be 'worthless', such as dense forest, is now often the centre of pharmaceutical and mineral 'mining', and 'carbon trading').

What should immediately strike the reader is the fact that almost all these settlements reflect colonial and imperial intent: locate the resource, set up a structure to exploit the resource, facilitate the resource's value to European endeavour. What were initially small nodal points at, in Neva Makgetla and Ann Seidman's (1980) words, 'the outposts of monopoly capitalism' are today massive conurbations, the size of which no one could possibly have foreseen even 50 years ago. While being located at the top of a watershed (e.g., Johannesburg, Maseru, Bulawayo, Harare, Windhoek) or at the bottom of a drainage basin (e.g., Cape Town, Durban, Dar es Salaam, Luanda) creates its own problems of supply and demand (as related to, for example, quantity, quality, seasonality, runoff, infiltration, wastewater treatment and disposal), these problems are magnified multifold when combined with (1) unanticipated rapid and continuous population growth; (2) a narrow economic profile; (3) dependence on a wasting asset or a group of resources that are readily substitutable; (4) municipal infrastructure designed for 1/10 or 1/20 of the present population; (5) limited financial, technical and human resources at the municipal level; and (6) central governments whose elected officials' primary interests lie elsewhere. Such is the case with almost every human settlement across southern Africa.

Vulnerabilities

Societies are vulnerable to many things. While there may be strength in numbers, and while no individual alone can guarantee that his or her needs are met, the 'collective' itself creates vulnerabilities. People clustered together create strengths – e.g., 'economies of scale' – but also weaknesses, as urban density requires efficient waste management, transportation, health services and policing, among other things. The inability to provide one or more of these collective goods can result in a cascade of problems related to health, peace and security.

American University professor James Mittelman (1988) argued that the state is the only social form capable of accumulating capital to the extent necessary to ensure the safety and wellbeing of millions of citizens. While capital is not the full measure of state capability – nor can money on its own guarantee peace and security – it is the fundamental basis for social order (or disorder) in a capitalist world system. How you make money, how you spend it, for what reason, where and why is the basis for global 'league tables' such as those compiled by the World Bank (i.e., World Development Report) and UNDP (i.e., Human Development Report).

During Africa's first wave of independence in the late 1950s and early 1960s, African leaders accepted the borders laid out at Berlin more than 75 years earlier. Schooled mainly in Europe, these children of modernisation clearly accepted the idea that as African states 'developed' and became 'modern', traditional social ties such as ethnicity would be displaced or overlain by cross-ethnic interests and allegiances born of modernisation: unions, professional associations, and the like. Similarly, they accepted the Rostowian 'take-off into sustained growth' arguments whereby certain leading sectors, fostered through development assistance, would transform 'traditional society and economy' into modern industrialised entities. Such ahistorical assumptions placed too much emphasis on agency – that decision-makers acting rationally could overturn centuries-old structures of resource exploitation. Such analysis also overplayed the autonomy of sovereign states (i.e., that they are not enmeshed in a cobweb of international relations) while underplaying the competitiveness and hierarchy of the system of states itself. Nkrumah's hopeful epithet masked the facts of life at the bottom of this hierarchy, and as near weightless entities with little or no pull in a cobweb dominated at the time by the United States and the Soviet Union. In this setting, 'development' and 'modernisation' should rather be seen as contextual frameworks within which dominant actors set about trying to order the world after their own interests and minor actors scrambled for attention. For southern African states and especially peoples, the move from colonialism to the Cold War was out of the frying pan and into the fire. To be sure, China, the Soviet Union and Cuba assisted importantly in the liberation struggles against colonial, settler and apartheid rule. But the United States and several 'sanctions busters' such as Israel, helped prolong these struggles, setting the entire region onto its present course. History shows that while pledging allegiance to one side or the other – capitalism or communism – sometimes facilitated useful developments (e.g., hydropower, import substitution), it more often attracted wars by proxy and a bad lot of authoritarian rulers, some of whom are still in place, having long outlived their 'best before' dates.

If the effects of colonialism and the Cold War were not enough to bring Africa's 'new states' to their knees, successive waves of global economic crises and the neoliberal response from state houses in the West certainly did. While the 1980s were dubbed 'the lost decade' in Africa, to be honest, it has been nearly 35 years of turmoil. As Table 2.1 shows, SADC states' Human Development Indices (HDIs) have barely moved from 1980's level.

The legacies of colonialism, the Cold War and three decades of economic structural adjustment on present-day realities in the region are clear: dysfunctional, extraverted states dependent on rents from wasting assets or minimally beneficiated raw materials, dualistic economies where the vast majority of the population is mired in a poverty trap though they work night and day while the 1 per cent hunker down behind high walls, and cities designed for tens of thousands are now home to millions.

Tables 2.1 and 2.2 present some summary data in relation to the SADC states. Based on UNDP data, Mauritius (ranked 72 on the Human Development Index, HDI) is the lone SADC state considered to have 'high human development'. Botswana, Namibia, South Africa and Swaziland all fall within the 'medium human development' ranking, while the rest remain mired at the bottom of the UNDP's HDI tables. While all states except South Africa and Zimbabwe have shown improvements over the last 30 years, one must acknowledge that these are marginal improvements at best. Mauritius and Botswana are the only SADC states with per capita Gross National Incomes (GNIs) (2008 data based on purchasing power parity) greater than $10,000. This may be compared to the top three countries in the rankings: Norway with $94,759, Australia with $47,370 and New Zealand with $30,439.

SADC states have difficulty in accumulating capital at a scale sufficient for making significant inroads into poverty alleviation. This is primarily because of their relatively undifferentiated economies. This does not mean, however, that they do not have robust sectors of the economy; neither does it mean that everyone is having difficulty. As is well known, several SADC states (South Africa, Namibia, Zambia, Zimbabwe) are among the most unequal states on earth, as measured by the Gini coefficient of income inequality. There is a great deal of money to be made in mining, commercial farming, transportation, security and insurance. Countries at the lowest end of the HDI show an overwhelming reliance on agriculture's contribution to GDP. As shown in Table 2.2, Tanzania, DRC, Malawi, Mozambique and Zambia are all heavily reliant on agriculture. At the same time, manufactures as a percentage of total exports remain very low: Zambia, 8 per cent; Malawi, 10 per cent; Mozambique, 12 per cent; Tanzania, 25 per cent. This may be compared to the two largest economies in the world, the United States (67 per cent) and China (94 per cent). South Africa is something of an anomaly. Even though 47 per cent of South Africa's total exports are manufactured goods, there is a very high import component in these goods (one might make a similar argument about China), thus making this sector vulnerable to foreign exchange values, global economic downturns, the value of gold (a major South African forex earner) and so on.

The value of the HDI is in its ability to illustrate in a relatively simple manner how states spend money in areas known to be crucial to (individual and collective) human development: education and health. So, beyond accumulating capital, the important question for a society is: What does a state do with that money (measured as GNI per capita, or GDP per capita) once it has access to it? As shown in Table 2.2, there is a direct correlation between states dependent upon agriculture for GDP and the inability to supply ready access to potable water and, especially, improved sanitation.

Table 2.1   Selected indicators for SADC states: HDI (1980, 2000, 2010) and GNI per capita (2008)

Country	2010 HDI rank	2010 HDI value	1980 HDI	2000 HDI	GNI/pc $ (PPP) 2008
Angola	146	.403	–	.349	4 941
Botswana	98	.633	.431	.572	1 204
DRC	168	.239	.267	.201	291
Lesotho	141	.427	.397	.423	2 021
Malawi	153	.385	.258	.344	911
Mauritius	72	.701	.525	.657	13 344
Mozambique	165	.284	.195	.224	854
Namibia	105	.606	–	.568	6 323
South Africa	110	.597	–	.634 (1995)	9 812
Swaziland	121	.498	–	.490	5 132
Tanzania	148	.398	–	.332	1 344
Zambia	150	.395	.382	.345	1 359
Zimbabwe	169	.140	.241	.232	76

Source: UNDP (2012).

Table 2.2 Selected indicators for SADC states

Country	Population 2010 (millions)	Per cent urban 2010	No access to water (per cent)	No access to sanitation (per cent)	Manufacturing per cent of total exports	Value added: Agriculture	Value added: Industry	Value added: Services
Angola	19	58.5	50	43	–	10	54	36
Botswana	2	61.1	5	40	–	–	–	–
DRC	67.8	35.2	54	77	–	43	24	33
Lesotho	2.1	26.9	15	71	–	–	–	–
Malawi	15.7	19.8	20	44	10	36	21	44
Mauritius	1.3	41.8	1	9	–	–	–	–
Mozambique	23.4	38.4	53	83	12	29	24	47
Namibia	2.2	38.0	8	67	–	–	–	–
South Africa	50.5	61.7	9	23	47	3	31	66
Swaziland	1.2	21.4	31	45	–	–	–	–
Tanzania	45.0	26.4	46	76	25	45	17	37
Zambia	13.3	35.7	40	51	8	21	58	21
Zimbabwe	12.6	38.3	18	56	34	–	–	–

Source: UNDP (2012).

Hidden from these tables is the fact that in these agriculture-dependent economies most of this value-added is generated by commercial agriculture that is highly mechanised in form and/or dependent on seasonal, migrant (and often expatriate) labour. In most SADC countries, the majority of rural people practise subsistence agriculture, participating in local, informal markets, and/or selling cash crops to larger producers or the state. In some countries, this type of farming accounts for as much as 80 per cent of total employment. The stability of the rural areas, moreover, depends on remittances home from family members engaged in money-making activities in cities (often in another country). Wedged onto marginally productive, dwindling pieces of communal land, smallholders are hemmed in as land is regazetted by the state either as 'freehold' or long-term (often 99 years) 'leasehold' and sold off to the highest bidder. As global market forces place further pressures on states to privatise more and more land, rural youth flee to the cities.

As shown in Table 2.2, SADC states are urbanising; indeed, they are urbanising at dramatic rates. Given the state's relative weakness (e.g., Malawi, Tanzania, Zambia), its ineptness (e.g., Zimbabwe, Lesotho), and its questionable values (e.g., Mozambique, Angola, Swaziland), the continuing shortfall of capital and skills to deliver urban services compounds already existing problems not only of poverty and personal insecurity, but of the stability of the state itself. As citizens turn to self-help (e.g., township warlords providing personal security; street vendors providing water; urban agriculture providing food; and the black market providing almost everything else), the gulf between state and civil society widens. So, 'pulling together' in the face of a shared challenge becomes even more difficult than it already is.

Something new out of Africa

In chaos one finds not only a sort of order, but also creativity. This early part of the twenty-first century may also be providing space for creativity. While the never-ending American 'war on terror' continues, the United States' desire for pockets of regional stability does give policy space to African leaders in stable states that was absent during most of the latter part of the twentieth century. Few have shown a willingness to take it, but it is nevertheless there. The democratic interregnum, imperfect as it is across SADC states, importantly gives voice to groups of people who were only too happy to 'exit' – avoiding the state at all costs – only a decade ago. These penetrated political systems, with their dense networks of global civil society groups, private sector actors, Intergovernmental Organisations (IGOs) and state 'partners', are also admitting of a much richer form of decision-making, governance even, than was typical in more recent times. By no means do they pull in the same direction; but that there is a sort of conversation going on at all seems to me to present opportunities for innovation and change. China's emergence out of globalisation has been much debated. On one hand, the West has criticised the way in which bilateral agreements have been made, suggesting a return to authoritarianism. On the other hand, African leaders applaud the generous terms and absence of political and economic cross-conditionalities typical of Western 'aid' and finance. More money, more roads, more jobs. Without doubt, there will also be a fair share of 'more white elephants' and 'more support for questionable leaders', such as those in Angola and Zimbabwe. But it does mean more options, and in a more open, democratic or quasi-democratic context there can be discussions about what exactly should be done for 'the greater good'. The same may be said for the latest run on resources.

Of course, it could all go pear-shaped. The constellation of forces arrayed around southern Africa's state forms looks suspiciously like a comprador elite. But, if we recognise and acknowledge this, rather than accept liberal tropes regarding improved management, transparent governance and human resource capacity-building as the necessary means for getting out from underdevelopment, it seems to me that we can more effectively look for ways into the system – development by stealth, if you will. As will be shown in the next chapter, in my view, water resources development and management offers one such productive avenue.

3

Seeing Water

How Much Water Is There, for Whom and What?

According to the World Water Development Report 4 (WWDR IV 2012), natural variability in physical phenomena and incomplete knowledge are the primary sources of uncertainty in water management in Africa. In this chapter, I review the ways and means of seeing water in Africa. As shown here, there is a variety of conceptual and technical innovations that both help and hinder our understanding of how much water there is and what it might be used for. From the perspective of the water engineer, water can always be found. Indeed, we inhabit 'the blue planet', and generally when we think of water we think of that which we see in ponds, streams, rivers, lakes, even puddles after a rainstorm. This is blue water, or surface water. It is fresh, meaning that is salt free, though it may be heavily mineralised, and in its pristine condition we can drink it. It not only refreshes us, but replenishes us as well. If we extend the definition of 'blue water' to 'all readily accessible freshwater', then this would also include the extensive groundwater resources that lie stored and/or moving beneath our feet.

Water is both a stock and a flow. As a stock, it may be permanently locked in glaciers or deep underground aquifers or be exposed to the elements in the form of freshwater lakes laid down during the last Ice Age. When such a store is tapped, and the water is withdrawn, we are said to be 'mining water', meaning that we are drawing down a fixed amount that will never be replenished and once we have withdrawn all of the resource we must search for another source. In relation to the management of water, a primary challenge is to determine the rate at which an aquifer is replenished through rainfall, and to then withdraw the water at a rate equal to or less than the rate of replenishment. Similarly, if we withdraw surface water at a rate greater than it will be replenished, we may well turn a flow – in other words, a resource that renews itself – into a stock. The Aral Sea and Lake Chad are two well-known cases. And while there is a plan to 'Save Lake Chad', some scholars believe that there may be such an effect as 'peak ecological water' whereby once past a certain threshold, an ecosystem may be completely and irrevocably transformed from one system (e.g., a wetland) into another (e.g., a desert or dryland).

Most of our planning decisions revolve around this 'blue water bias'. However, water comes in many colours:

- Blue: readily accessible surface and groundwater
- Grey: non-sewerage, household water that may be recycled for other purposes
- Brown: industrial water that is generally free of toxic chemicals
- Black (or Purple): industrial water that is heavily polluted with toxic substances and is unlikely to be rehabilitated for other uses or safe to reintroduce to the system; sewerage water is included here but new technologies may be applied to turn sewerage water into potable water (so we may well need a new colour to describe this)
- Green: evapotranspiration – in other words, water that either passes through the root zone of a plant and is transpired in the production of biomass or is evaporated back into the atmosphere without producing biomass. Falkenmark and Rockstrom (2004) further separate these into productive and unproductive green water flows.

Grey, brown and black water are really just blue water transformed. Only in the case of black water is it lost to the system, or if introduced into the system does it pose a serious health threat to the biotic community. Green water, however, should grab our attention, for it is this water that is underplayed in all calculations regarding resource abundance/ scarcity. I will return to this point after briefly describing water in Africa.

Water resources in Africa

Water resources and their availability vary greatly, both spatially and temporally, across the length and breadth of the African continent. We can imagine the continent's dominant climate zones as a series of concentric circles radiating outward from a central core. The central core (West/Central Africa) is the humid region with average annual rainfall greater than 1600 mm/year and occurring throughout the year. Surrounding this core is the sub-humid region with distinct wet and dry seasons and average rainfall of 800 to 1 600 mm/year. Substantial rainfall in the rainy season(s) is offset by almost no precipitation during the dry season(s). Beyond the sub-humid region are the semi-arid regions (the savannas), with average rainfall of 400 to 800 mm/year. Rainfall has a high interannual variability, with the coefficient of variation being greater than 30 per cent. Africa is also home to extensive desert regions, or arid to hyper-arid zones: the Sahara in the north, and the Namib-Kalahari in the south. The extreme northern part of Africa and some of the areas at high altitude, such as the eastern highlands in Zimbabwe, have a temperate climate.

The seasonal variation of rainfall in Africa is due to the annual north-south migration of the Inter-Tropical Convergence Zone (ITCZ). Interannual variation of rainfall is partly explained by the occurrence of El Niño and La Niña events, with all of southern Africa being dramatically impacted by these occurrences. Most parts of Africa are located within the tropical region, receiving large amounts of solar radiation, resulting in warm to high temperatures. This abundance of solar radiation and generally high temperatures, together with low humidity through most parts of Africa, result in very high evaporation rates, so-called 'evaporative demand'. According to Mamdouh Shahin (2002), annual average reference evapotranspiration rates vary from 1 000–1 400 mm/year in the humid equatorial region and 1 400–2 000 mm/year in the semi-arid region to 2 000–3 000 mm/year in the arid regions.

Evapotranspiration rates exceed rainfall during most of the months in the semi-arid region, which restricts successful production of rain-fed crops. High evapotranspiration rates cause significant loss of water from surface water bodies. Shahin, of the International Institute for Hydraulic and Environmental Engineering in the Netherlands, has estimated that 80 per cent of the rain falling over Africa returns to the atmosphere through evapotranspiration. The combination of highly seasonal rainfall and high evapotranspiration rates results in most rivers drying up during the dry season, which limits the amount of water readily and easily available for human and wildlife use. According to Shahin, the proportion of rainfall forming runoff, the runoff coefficient, generally varies from 1 per cent in the arid deserts and 5–20 per cent in the semi-arid region to 20–50 per cent in the humid equatorial region.

The southern Africa region has a mean annual runoff of 57 mm/ year, and the annually renewable water resources range from 1 000 to 2 000 m³/capita/year for most countries. Of course, these figures vary greatly both across and within countries. As shown in Table 3.1, while the Democratic Republic of Congo (DRC) has a rainfall-to-runoff (including groundwater recharge) rate of 4:1, in Botswana the ratio is 100:1, and in South Africa, the region's heaviest water user and most industrialised country, the total annually available water resources relative to rainfall is less than 7 per cent. What this means, in part, is that the region – like the continent – is heavily dependent upon rain-fed agricultural production. Whereas there is much potential for increased irrigation, the real challenge is to decrease evaporation and enhance transpiration, particularly through food crops: what Falkenmark and Rockstrom (2004) call 'vapour shift' or achieving 'more crop per drop'.

There are extensive groundwater resources across the African continent. Groundwater is particularly important for water security in Africa where the majority of the population lives in small and dispersed settlements in rural areas. Due to the costs of installing and maintaining water treatment and distribution systems, the provision of water to most of these dispersed rural populations from surface water bodies is

Table 3.1 SADC precipitation and internally renewable water resources

Country	Precipitation mm/yr	Area of country (,000 ha)	Precipitation km³/yr	Surface water internal km³/yr	Groundwater internal km³/yr	Overlap km³/yr	Total internal renew km³/yr
Angola	1 010	124 670	1259.000	145.000	58.000	55.00	148.000
Botswana	416	58 173	242.990	0.800	1.700	0.10	2.400
DRC	1 543	234 486	3618.000	899.000	421.000	420.00	900.000
Lesotho	788	3 036	23.920	5.230	0.500	0.50	5.230
Malawi	1 181	11 848	139.900	16.140	2.500	2.50	16.140
Mauritius	2 041	204	4.164	2.358	.893	.50	2.751
Mozambique	1 032	79 938	825.000	97.300	17.000	14.00	100.300
Namibia	285	82 429	234.900	4.100	2.100	0.04	6.160
South Africa	495	121 909	603.400	43.000	4.800	3.00	44.800
Swaziland	788	1 736	13.680	2.640	0.660	0.66	2.640
Tanzania	1 071	94 730	1015.000	80.000	30.000	26.00	84.000
Zambia	1 020	75 261	767.700	80.200	47.000	47.00	80.200
Zimbabwe	657	39 076	256.700	11.260	6.000	5.00	20.000

Source: FAO Aquastat, www.fao.org/nr/water/aquastat/main/index.stm (accessed 23–24 July 2013).

not economically viable. Groundwater, however, has several advantages with regard to the provision of potable water to rural populations in Africa. It generally lacks microbiological contamination and therefore does not require investment in water treatment systems. Furthermore, groundwater is often locally available to supply these dispersed rural populations. During times of drought, groundwater is often the only available resource in rural areas. The availability of groundwater mainly depends on the nature of the geology of an area. According to Alan MacDonald and Jeff Davies (2000), the geological formations of Africa can be classified into the following categories for the purpose of describing the potential for groundwater occurrence: (1) Precambrian basement complex consisting of crystalline and metamorphic rocks, (2) volcanic rocks, (3) consolidated sediments and (4) unconsolidated sediments. Crystalline and metamorphic rocks of the basement complex occupy about a third of Africa, and are generally inherently impermeable. Groundwater only occurs where these rocks have been weathered and fractured, with the depth of weathering greatly determining the yield of aquifers. The depth of weathering tends to be a few metres in arid regions and as deep as 90 metres in humid regions. The amount of water available increases with the depth of weathering. Aquifers occurring within the basement complex are generally capable of supporting water supply systems for rural domestic water use and small-scale irrigation. Consolidated sediments mainly comprise sandstone, limestone, siltstone and mudstone and occupy about 32 per cent of the land area in sub-Saharan Africa. The Karoo and Kalahari sediments in southern Africa are some of the important formations in this category. Sandstones generally contain aquifers with very large amounts of water. As described in World Water Development Report IV (2012), the Nubian Sandstone aquifer that underlies Chad, Libya, Sudan and Egypt is estimated to be 2 million km^2 in area and contains approximately 150 000–450 000 km^3 of fossil water, laid down 30 000 years ago during the last Ice Age. Fractured limestone also has the potential to store large amounts of water. The most productive aquifers occur in unconsolidated sediments, which

> **Box 2.1   Groundwater for water security in Northern Namibia?**
>
> 'A new aquifer, called Ohangwena II, has been found in northern Namibia. The vast water deposit straddles the border between Namibia and Angola – on the Namibian side, it covers about 1 075 square miles. According to Martin Quinger, a project manager from the German Federal Institute for Geoscience and Natural Resources, this is a monumental find. The amount of stored water would equal the current supply of this area in northern Namibia for 400 years, which has about 40 per cent of the population, he said to the BBC. In Namibia, finding an aquifer is akin to striking gold. The country's land is the driest in all of sub-Saharan Africa, and the continent as a whole is already seeing widespread droughts due to climate change. An aquifer is basically a subterraneous chunk of land that is saturated with groundwater. That groundwater can be accessed by wells, although removing it can be risky since aquifers can run dry if too much water is demanded at once. What we are aiming at is a sustainable water supply so we only extract the amount of water that is being recharged, said Quinger. And Namibia's aquifer comes with special risks of its own. This trove of fresh groundwater has a smaller aquifer of saltwater sitting right on top of it, and mixing the two would compromise the quality of this valuable find. If people don't comply with our technical recommendations they might create a hydraulic shortcut between the two aquifers, which might lead to the salty water from the upper one contaminating the deep one or vice versa, Quinger explained. If all goes well, this could be a fantastic find for Namibia.'
>
> Source: http://www.ibtimes.com/namibiapercentE2percent80percent99s-miraculous-
> wellspring-newly-discovered-aquifer-could-help-develop-agriculture-730013

occupy large areas of Chad and the DRC, as well as the coastal areas of Nigeria, Namibia and Kenya.

Scarcity

A great deal of academic and policy literature seems to focus on the prospect of Africa 'running out of water'; or, put differently, of supply not meeting demand and so igniting a host of problems including inter-state competition and possibly violent conflict. Within the SADC region, the Zambezi Basin has been identified as a 'basin at risk' by Aaron Wolf and his colleagues (2003) at Oregon State University who compile the Transboundary Freshwater Dispute Database (TFDD). The empirical grounding of these analyses is a scarcity index first developed by Malin Falkenmark in 1986, and since modified by Falkenmark and Rockstrom (2004), among others. The water scarcity index, relabelled a 'water crowding index' in their 2004 study, is a simple calculation of people per 'flow unit', with a flow unit equal to 1 million cubic metres per year. Given that people, on average, require $1\ 700\ m^3/yr$ of water, then a system is said to have sufficient water up to a maximum of 600 people per flow unit. The 'flow' is determined by a country's total available renewable freshwater resources. According to Falkenmark and Rockstrom (2004), where there is less than $1\ 700\ m^3/capita/yr$ of freshwater available, or more than 600 people per flow unit, a country is said to suffer from 'water stress'; at less than $1\ 000\ m^3/capita/yr$ of freshwater available or more than $1\ 000$ people per flow unit, a country is said to suffer 'chronic water scarcity'; and at less than $500\ m^3/capita/yr$, or more than $2\ 000$ people per flow unit, a country is living 'beyond the water barrier'.

Feeling this to offer only a partial view, Falkenmark and Rockstrom (2004), added two other variables to give a more complete picture of water resource vulnerability: technical water scarcity and an index on aridity (measuring evaporative demand). Technical water scarcity measures blue water utilisation – in other words, the percentage of freshwater withdrawn for use relative to its total availability. Their benchmark is Europe, where evidence shows that once a society has reached a blue water withdrawal of about 20 per cent of total available water, any additional exploitation of the resource places stress on available financial and technical resources. The aridity index matters because where countries may have the same amount of rainfall per annum, the available freshwater measured as runoff and as soil moisture – in other words, water that soaks into the ground becoming available in the root zone of plants rather than evaporating back to the atmosphere – will be far less in the arid or semi-arid zone country than the one in the temperate zone, so limiting use options and complicating management practices. They label this vulnerability 'green water scarcity'. Bringing these factors together, the authors suggest that a country in an ecological zone with high evaporative demand, with more than 600 persons per flow unit and with more than 20 per cent of their blue water mobilised, is particularly vulnerable to water management problems and issues. Within the context of climate change and the uncertainties surrounding hydrological cycles, it is imperative that coping capabilities be enhanced. In the view of Leif Ohlsson and Anthony Turton (1999), many of these countries, however, suffer from 'second order resource scarcities', meaning that they lack the social and institutional frameworks necessary to assist them to overcome 'first order' – i.e., the resource itself – problems and scarcities. In the view of the International Water Management Institute, most SADC states suffer only 'second order' types of scarcity (see, e.g., Rijsberman, 2006).

Based on Falkenmark and Rockstrom's (2004) conceptualisation of scarcity, and using data from the World Bank, it can be seen in Table 3.2 that no SADC state suffers 'technical stress', all having withdrawals well below their indicator of <20 per cent withdrawn relative to total freshwater available. At the same time, both South Africa and Zimbabwe would be said to suffer 'chronic water scarcity', while Botswana and Malawi would be said to suffer 'water stress'. As shown in Chapter 1, there are large populations clustered in arid and semi-arid regions (Johannesburg, Cape Town, Bulawayo, Gaborone, Windhoek) or in regions of significant seasonal water scarcity. These are also areas that often suffer drought and flood, so 'green water scarcity' should be regarded as a relative concept. At the same time, all SADC states show significant decreases in freshwater availability, so reflecting the high rates of population growth in the region.

Compounding the issue of scarcity is the fugitive nature of water and the number of shared river basins in the SADC. As shown in Table 3.3, only the island state of Mauritius is 100 per cent dependent upon its 'own' water. Most SADC states show a significant dependency on external surface water (shown as a percentage of total renewable freshwater) (see Chapter 5).

Table 3.2   SADC freshwater availability per capita and withdrawals as percentage of total availability

Country	Freshwater availability (m³/cap/yr) 1980–2	Freshwater availability (m³/cap/yr) 2008–12	Freshwater withdrawals as per cent of total availability 2008–12
Angola	18 071	7 334	0.6
Botswana	2 240	1 208	0.2
DRC	32 412	14 078	0.6
Lesotho	3 806	2 577	0.1
Malawi	2 461	1 044	1.0
Mauritius	2 777	2 139	0.7
Mozambique	7 879	4 080	0.7
Namibia	5 829	2 778	0.3
South Africa	1 546	886	12.5
Swaziland	4 129	2 178	1.0
Tanzania	4 222	1 812	5.2
Zambia	12 862	5 882	1.7
Zimbabwe	1 556	918	4.2

Source: http://data.worldbank.org/indicator/ER.H20.FWTL.K3; http://data.worldbank.org/ indicator/ER.H20.INTRO.PC (accessed 28 July 2013).

Running out of water?

The policy and academic worlds are awash with studies that accept the above analysis without question. It is almost standard practice to begin, as the World Water Development Report IV (WWDR IV 2012) and the Intergovernmental Panel on Climate Change (IPCC) chapter on Africa (Niang et al. 2014) do, with a narrative that begins by pointing out that though the continent has a great deal of water, millions of people lack adequate access to potable water and sanitation. These studies then quickly move to a juxtaposition of climatological and physiological facts (e.g., high evaporative demand and extreme events) with the facts of demographic change (especially high population growth and the move

Table 3.3   SADC surface water flows, treaty water, total renewable water and surface water dependency

Country	Surface water IN and boundary km³/yr	Surface water OUT km³/yr	Not subject to treaty km³/yr	Total renewable km³/yr	Dependency on external surface water (per cent)
Angola	119.00	0.00	All	148.000	0.000
Botswana	9.04	0.00	All	12.240	80.390
DRC	383.00	2.00	All	1283.000	29.850
Lesotho	0.00	5.20	2.992	3.022	0.000
Malawi	1.14	16.14	All	16.140	6.597
Mauritius	0.00	0.00	0	2.751	0.000
Mozambique	116.80	0.00	All	217.100	53.800
Namibia	11.56	12.00	All	17.720	65.240
South Africa	6.60	10.40	2.208 IN/ 9.3 OUT	51.400	12.840
Swaziland	1.87	4.50	All	4.510	41.460
Tanzania	12.84	12.27	All	96.270	12.750
Zambia	25.00	105.20	All	105.200	23.760
Zimbabwe	7.74	11.26	All	20.000	38.700

Source: FAO Aquastat, www.fao.org/nr/water/aquastat/main/index.stm
(accessed 23–24 July 2013).

to the cities) in order to suggest that there is not enough water because there are too many people. It is not my intention to deny the importance of any of these factors. To the contrary, taken together they constitute a nettlesome confluence of water-related challenges.

My issue is with both the accuracy of the claims regarding scarcity, and with the broad policy avenues they open up. Let's start with the measurement of 'scarcity'. Table 3.2 shows availability of freshwater resources per capita per SADC state, offering comparisons over

30 years. It also shows current estimates of total withdrawals relative to total availability. What is suggested here, among other things, is (1) relative abundance of water resources in the northern half of southern Africa; but (2) large per capita declines across the board; (3) chronic water scarcity in South Africa and in most of the basins shared by the state; and (4) no technical water scarcity anywhere in the region. The picture framed for policy-makers is, then, looming scarcities that may possibly be addressed through large-scale water infrastructure projects. The shared nature of the resource suggests the relevance of a regional approach and, given the need for a technical solution, South African leadership. Indeed, as discussed in Chapter 5, this is exactly the approach being taken, with a heavy dose of international state, civil society and private sector involvement rolled into the mix.

Are we seeing water clearly? One consequence of the blue water bias is that green water remains invisible. In the words of Falkenmark and Rockstrom (2004):

This water blindness is quite fascinating. In view of the rapidly growing world population, and the warnings from environmentalists that large-scale expansion of irrigation will be unacceptable, it is absolutely essential to focus on the invisible water in the soil that is necessary for plant production.

In addition, they state that 'it is not widely known that about 60 per cent of rainfall stems from vapour produced from the land surface. This means that the hydrological "bloodstream" that supports the biosphere and the anthroposphere is, to a large extent, generated by the biosphere itself'. I find it intriguing that these two authors who place such important emphasis on green water nevertheless fall into the trap of arguing 'scarcity' through 'freshwater availability' – i.e., blue water biased – data. In my view, it is imperative that we not only see the invisible/green water, but also how the water we have is used both by humans and by nature if we are to have a complete picture of the management options available to us.

To begin, we must acknowledge that 'freshwater withdrawals' is a measure of relative value when attached to daily per capita needs. In a region primarily dependent upon green water and/or virtual water trade for food security, 'freshwater availability' only matters in relation to direct domestic, commercial and industrial needs, i.e., 'small water'. At minimum, 'freshwater availability relative to population' should be adjusted to account for the green water embedded in food consumption – in other words, about 80 per cent of individual water needs. Not only is it a crude measure at best; it also leads us to a narrow range of policy options due to 'the facts' of existing or impending scarcity. For example, we have noted above that, technically, southern Africa suffers no water scarcity. It is understandable, therefore, that organisations such as IWMI argue that the region suffers 'economic water scarcity' as opposed to physical scarcity. In Turton's view (2008), this 'second order scarcity' is what must be addressed if the region is to enjoy water security. As a general point, I agree with him. But the basis for the claim is suspect. For example, if South Africa approaches the 40 per cent threshold of acute technical scarcity, should South Africans feel as though their limits have been reached? I ask this because rarely do we see in the global South any comparative data from the global North. During 2008–12, US withdrawals as percentage of total renewable freshwater were 478.4 per cent, down from 517 per cent 30 years earlier. China's withdrawals were 554 per cent, up from 443 per cent in 1980–82, and India's 761 per cent, up from 438 per cent in the same period. Including, as it does, mined water from non-renewable aquifers, reuse and desalinisation, the statistic obfuscates as much as it enlightens. Is the US running out of water, or is it incredibly efficient? This is the trouble with aggregate statistics; they do not give a clear picture of what is happening on the ground, especially where water is concerned.

Even if we focus on the watershed/basin, a focus on withdrawals says little about a number of very important issues relating to availability, access, use and management:

- Presenting a ratio of available renewable freshwater relative to population is grossly misleading, in part because most people across sub-Saharan Africa are dependent on rainfall for their food production (big water – in other words, from 600 to 1 300 m³/cap/yr)

- Withdrawals are a general category and say nothing about what the water is being used for and who benefits from its use. So to claim that a river basin is 'closed' or 'near closure', meaning that there can be no further allocations, deflects investigation of current use profiles. One such investigation, conducted by James Cullis and Barbara van Koppen in 2009, revealed that in the Olifants River of South Africa, the Gini coefficient of water use inequality is 0.96, revealing that 99.5 per cent of rural households directly use 5 per cent of water withdrawn. When adjusted for water benefits (as measured through employment) the Gini coefficient falls to 0.63, mirroring almost perfectly the overall Gini coefficient in income equality for South Africa at that time (0.64). Obviously, benefits from current withdrawals are badly skewed toward the already empowered.

- To show that available freshwater is decreasing (see Table 3.3) is simply another way of saying population is increasing relative to blue water availability. Most rural people are dependent upon rain-fed agriculture and draw their household water or water their stock from shallow wells, meaning that they are completely 'off the grid'; does this mean that they are water insecure? Does this mean that they wouldn't benefit from a reallocation of currently withdrawn water that is used to grow commercial cotton for export? In both cases, the answer is no.

- According to calculations made by Falkenmark and Rockstrom (2004), domestic water needs are only 2 per cent of total human water demands. The lack of it has very little to do with declining levels of available freshwater; rather, it is a serious political issue that tells us a great deal about state-civil society relations in a particular place and time.

- Country-level and basin-level freshwater availability analysis also fails to consider the movement of virtual water in and out of the basin. South Africa is a net exporter of virtual water. Given the Gini coefficient of income inequality highlighted above, this raises questions about uses and beneficiaries along the entire blue/green water-production value chain.
- Crop choice matters with regard to available water. There may be gross inefficiencies of water use by growing C_3 crops in climatological zones better suited for C_4 crops,[2] but there may be huge markets (and therefore profits and taxes) for these crops (wheat, barley, rye, oats), leading governments and the private sector to 'push the ecological envelope' – compensating for climate through intensive irrigation and application of fertilisers – to the detriment of local-level food security.
- A great deal of the water that is withdrawn goes into food crops that simply rot either in the fields, or en route to market or at the market itself. This water will simply renew itself either within the existing basin, or as an out of basin transfer, but the ultimate benefit of the food is never realised.
- The current use pattern in SADC states mirrors that of the wider world, with irrigation generally using between 60 and 80 per cent of all withdrawals (Botswana being an exception). Given the nature of beverage economies explored earlier, it is clear that most of this resource is used not to feed or clothe citizens of SADC states, but to enrich a small sector of large-holder commercial farmers, and generate revenues for those along the value chain, including the state, which will

---

2. C3 and C4 refer to differing light-independent reactions of photosynthesis involving carbon fixation in plants. C3 plants are generally associated with temperate zones, and C4 plants with tropical/sub-tropical/arid zones. C3 plants are incapable of closing their stomata (unlike C4 plants) and so are ill-suited to environments with long dry seasons.

take its cut through taxation. Granted, this tax money may assist the state in providing improved services and public goods (but it very well may not). The sector also provides (seasonal) limited employment (at usually less than $1/day) to thousands of people (many of whom are not citizens of the states in which they work). Can we then say that the water is put to good use? Perhaps, but it is certainly not the best use to which it could be put.

- In addition, the entire sector is impacted by local and global markets, state supports and subsidies, and the presence or absence of efficiencies. Marketing boards still function across the SADC, in service not of the farmer but of the state and the urban consumer. Farmers across the SADC are being encouraged to diversify into cash crops, shifting some of their small holdings out of food production. Data compiled by David Molden and colleagues (2007) at the Consultative Group for International Agricultural Research (CGIAR) shows that in Malawi, among other things, smallholder burley tobacco growers' incomes are more than two times greater than the incomes of food-crop producers in the poorest regions.
- Land ownership is also an important issue that rarely features in discussions regarding 'basin closure' or 'chronic water insecurity', but across southern Africa ownership is often at the heart of poverty and food insecurity, where people have been pushed onto small holdings while multinationals and major national commercial farmers dominate the best land, growing cash crops for export.
- Food preferences and changing diets are also invisible in most aggregate-statistics-based narratives about available water. Data in Allan's 2011 study of virtual water shows range-fed beef to have a much smaller water footprint than that of grain-fed beef, with the conversion rate being in the order of five to eight times as much water consumed to produce 1 000 kcal of meat relative to 1 000 kcal of vegetables. Cattle produced

in SADC for markets in Europe must abide by EU laws, so ensuring a much larger water use than cattle produced for local markets.

In my view, the shift away from the finite resource versus increasing population narrative is necessary if we are to be able to see water properly: in its various colours; where it is embedded in processes of production and consumption; how it travels physically and virtually; how it serves to unite and divide a society; how our use profiles have changed over time. The resource is ever renewable, so a 'scarcity' narrative, in my view, takes us nowhere toward sustainable, equitable and efficient structures of management and governance.

When we see water properly in all of its complexity, as I have tried to summarise here, a world of possibilities opens up to us. We are not bound to travel down the policy avenues opened up by first-order (physical) and second-order (institutional) scarcity analyses, with their heavy emphasis on supply-side interventions and large-scale institutional change. While they do offer insights, in my view they hide more than they reveal. The real challenges associated with water in the region, in my view, are to put it to uses that benefit everyone, that enhance the developmental choices and life chances of all. As it stands, my summary here suggests that far from a scarce resource, the rich have it in abundance while the poor do not. Since the rich make policy, it serves us ill to keep saying that we do not have enough water. To say this is to encourage them to hang on to the resource they have already captured, and to grab more whenever possible.

4

Using Water

Consumptive and Non-consumptive Water Use in the SADC States

The water-use profile of people around the world has hardly changed since the Neolithic revolution: blue water drawn from wells and rivers for food production, domestic needs, the extraction of raw materials, and the manufacture of goods of all kinds. Over time we have taken control of this resource and bent its natural ebb and flow to our will – too often with unintended negative consequences. Few are the social forms that follow the resource, that follow the natural patterns of the region. Even the Masaai and the San depend on government-supplied boreholes. As with the rest of the world, southern Africans continue to dam, drain and divert their water resources. This is the consumptive face of water use – which, technically speaking, is not really consumptive unless the water supply itself is ruined beyond repair (see Chapter 3). But we also use water non-consumptively – in other words, leave it where it manifests naturally, or where we have captured it for a parallel use such as hydropower, to enjoy it recreationally and often spiritually. In this chapter, I look briefly at the way we use water within the SADC states, describing the trends in legislation as they reflect changing perspectives and on-the-ground dynamics. The bulk of the chapter is devoted to water for domestic consumption: in cities and in small rural communities. As shown in Chapter 3, the vast majority of water consumed by citizens of SADC states comes embedded in food grown with green water. Water for personal use requires a tiny fraction of the region's annual needs. As stated previously, this is 'small water'. How is it, then, that small water causes such big problems? Let's find out.

Legislating 'use'

Prior to the end of colonial/imperial and apartheid rule in the SADC states, access and use of the region's water resources was codified in a series of laws and policies, most of which stemmed from the pre-independence period, were revised shortly after independence and were not looked at again until powerful dynamics were set in motion globally and locally at the end of the 1980s. As may be seen in Table 4.1, Botswana's current laws reflect both the earlier trend as well as Batswana policy-makers' reluctance to move too quickly on anything, irrespective of what their commitments to the SADC suggest they should be doing. So the Borehole Act stems from colonial rule (where the British wanted to keep a check on the key blue water resource in the country). This was followed by a new Water Act in the post-independence period and the creation of a water utility corporation reflecting trends and designs for urban development and water service delivery mechanisms.

All of the other SADC land-based member states have moved quickly to reform their water laws in line with emerging global best practice, initially in the period preceding the 1992 Earth Summit in Rio de Janeiro, but especially after that summit as the global focus on water resources governance and management really gained traction among developed states themselves (see Chapter 5).

All these laws reflect the desire to dispense with the private right to water, now uniformly defined as a publicly owned resource, held in trust for the nation through either the Constitution or through the head of state where that head of state is a king, such as Letsie III in Lesotho and Mswati III of Swaziland. Accompanying these new water laws and policies is a regionally adopted approach to managing water within the context of a river basin. Zimbabwe led the way by establishing Catchment Councils throughout the country in the late 1990s and early 2000s. Reflecting the central tenets of IWRM, water was to be managed at the lowest appropriate level, with management structures developed jointly by government and basin-wide stakeholders. So, most SADC states have developed Catchment Management Agencies (CMAs), or River Basin Authorities (RBAs), whose primary tasks are to implement

Table 4.1   Water laws in SADC member states

Country	Law and date	Comments
Angola	Water Law (Law 5/02) (2002)	
Botswana	Water Act (1968) Borehole Act (1956) Water Utilities Corporation Act (1970)	A National Water Master Plan was developed in 1991 and revised in 2006; there is a Draft Water Bill on the table since 2005
Democratic Republic of Congo	Water Act (2010)	
Lesotho	Water Act (2008)	
Malawi	Water Resources Act (2013)	Replaces the 1969 Water Act
Mauritius	River and Canal Act (1863) Groundwater Act (1970) Water Authority Act (1971) Irrigation Authority Act (1979)	
Mozambique	Water Law No.16/91 (1991)	
Namibia	Water Resources Management Act (2004) (Act No. 24)	Replaces the Water Act (Act No. 54) of 1956
South Africa	Water Act (1998) Water Services Act (1997)	
Swaziland	Water Act (2003)	
Tanzania	Water Resources Management Act (2009)	
Zambia	Water Resources Management Act (2011)	Repeals Water Act CAP 198 of 2006
Zimbabwe	The Water Act CAP 20:24 (1998) Zimbabwe National Water Authority Act CAP 20:25 (1998)	

Source: UCT Law Library website, http://www.law.lib.uct.ac.za/; various official government websites.

the goals and visions as articulated in national water policy, strategy and law. In theory these authorities are composed of sub-catchment and stream-level elements (water-user associations) that inform the decision-makers in the CMA regarding actions to be taken in their best interest. Those who sit at the head of the authority must then ensure that local wants and needs fit with the overall capacity of the basin to deliver water equitably, efficiently and sustainably. The vision among SADC state policy-makers is that the water management system will be self-contained and self-financing, developing its own basin management plan and funding activities through user-pay fees. Departments of water affairs, in their many variations across SADC states, will provide governance oversight, technical support, and engage in regulatory activities in line with existing policy and law.

Most SADC states have struggled with this new water architecture, primarily, in my view, due to the fact that the creation of a new seat of decision-making authority threatens to shift power away from where it had hitherto resided – with a central state agency – and possibly empower people at the political periphery in their own interests. Such an event would no doubt upset extant social relations within river basins, which have been long dominated by a few actors (irrigation boards and mines). Evidence shows resistance to the new water architecture to be legion across all SADC states, hence the co-presence of some of the best water policies and laws in the world, with some of the worst (i.e., socially inequitable, environmentally unsustainable, economically inefficient) practices. A 2016 special issue of *Water Alternatives*, edited by Lyla Mehta, Bill Derman and Emmanuel Manzungu, accurately captures these difficulties. How this water continues to be used is shown in Figure 4.1.

What is clear from this figure is the continuing dominance of blue water by agriculture, and by agriculture I mean irrigated big agriculture: sugar along the eastern flank of southern Africa; wine and fruit in South Africa's Western Cape; sunflowers and wheat in the Pandamatenga region of Botswana; tea and tobacco in Malawi; tobacco, tea, coffee and various fruits in Mozambique, Zambia and Zimbabwe; table grapes and sugar at either end of Namibia along the shores of the Orange-Senqu

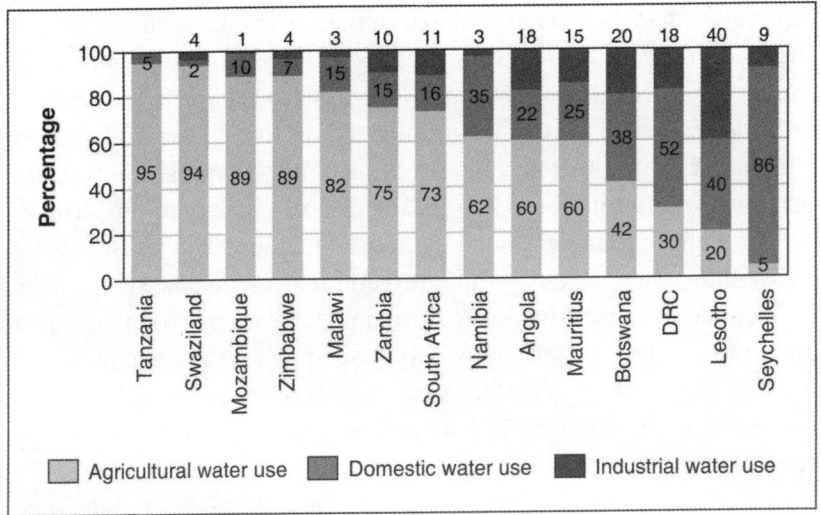

Figure 4.1   SADC water use by sector
Source: SADC (2012: 26).

and Okavango-Zambezi river systems; cotton, coffee, cashew nuts, tea and tobacco in Tanzania, for instance. The goal of most SADC states is to expand the land under irrigation; a key question, however, is how such expansion will widen the pool of beneficiaries. As reported by SADC in its Statistical Yearbook for 2014, a large proportion of the region's citizens live under national poverty lines, with a majority of these being rural dwellers.[3] Where data is available, only Mauritius (8.5 per cent) has less than 20 per cent of its people living below the poverty line. At the top end are Zimbabwe (72 per cent), Zambia (60.5 per cent; 78 per cent of rural dwellers), DRC (71.3 per cent), Swaziland (63 per cent; 73 per cent of rural dwellers), Madagascar (68.7 per cent), Mozambique (54.7 per cent), and Lesotho (56.6 per cent). Performing somewhat better are Tanzania (35.7 per cent), South Africa (22 per cent) and

---

3. http://www.sadc.int/information-services/sadc-statistics#Yearbook.

Botswana (20.7 per cent). Virtually all of those who reside in rural poverty share similar characteristics: they work the least naturally productive land; they depend on the rain for crop growth; they have limited access to government supports such as seed and fertiliser; and, in the age of HIV/AIDS, they are increasingly female-headed households. As suggested in Chapter 2, however, it seems that this serious and significant number of people is off government radar, preoccupied as they are with biofuels, land grabs, mining expansion, and so on.

The details of this story are beyond the scope of this book. In the balance of this chapter I will focus on water for cities. Water for domestic consumption constitutes a small fraction of all the water used in the world and the SADC is no different. Drinking water in particular should not be so difficult to deliver. Where people reside in cities, they are easily reached; where they reside in rural areas, sinking boreholes is not a complicated procedure. So why should anyone go without everyday dependable access to the amount of water they cannot do without?

Water for cities

Providing adequate water and sanitation for the world's urban masses is, in my view, the most important challenge of good governance of the twenty-first century. The future is urban. In fact, the present is urban: official estimates suggest that more than 50 per cent of humanity is now living in cities. Cities are facing very different sorts of challenges. Those that arose out of the so-called first demographic transition fostered by the Industrial Revolution face significant challenges related to aging infrastructure: how to repair it, replace it and upgrade it. This is primarily a so-called First-World problem. Those cities that have arisen out of the post-World War II, post-colonial second demographic transition face the primary challenge of meeting the needs of rapidly expanding populations that have over-stretched existing infrastructure and, in many cases, exist in a sort of parallel peri-urban space: part of the greater metropolitan area, but largely unacknowledged – except to be regarded as a major problem – to formal authorities.

The absolute number and percentage of people living in cities has increased dramatically over the last 60 years, with roughly half of all urban dwellers living in Asia. While Asia's urban population has dramatically risen as a percentage of total world urban population, percentages in Europe and North America have fallen significantly. In addition, the size of the world's largest cities is also increasing dramatically.

Southern Africa's early-modern cities were small, neo-European enclaves designed to serve the interests of a limited number of European traders, settlers and administrators, eventually emerging as functional nodes in service of the imperial enterprise: at the tops of watersheds as defensive structures (Harare, Bulawayo, Maseru) or at mine- or railheads (Johannesburg, Lusaka), at the coasts (Cape Town, Dar es Salaam, Maputo, Luanda, Durban) where the subcontinent's goods and people could be exported to the world, and the empire's manufactures could be imported for a captive market. Others were created simply for administrative purposes (Dodoma, Lilongwe, Gaborone, Mbabane). Windhoek began its life as a small settlement around a freshwater spring, later to serve as a defensive battlement in service of Germany's colonial interests (see also Chapter 2).

The central point to be made here is that were an urban planner to be shown a topographic map of southern Africa and asked to choose a site for a million-city, it is unlikely that more than two or three coastal settlements would have figured in her calculations. To 'prepare' Africans for independence, various 'big push' projects – in particular large dam building for hydropower and water supply, primarily for the newly created capital cities – were undertaken (see Table 4.2 and Figure 4.2). Yet no one could anticipate the scale of the influx into these small cities. According to data provided by Nigerian professor Tayo Odumosu in 2000, across sub-Saharan Africa, the number of people living in cities increased thirteen-fold between 1950 and 2000, from 33 million to 417 million. According to the World Water Development Report II (WWDR II 2006), an estimated 42.4 per cent of Africans lived in cities in 2000, in contrast to only 14.9 per cent 50 years earlier. The growth of cities derives from three trends: in-migration, natural increases, and expansion of the urban space into the surrounding hinterland. Data from the United Nations Population Fund (UNFPA, 2007) reveals that, in 1900, Africa had no cities with a population of one million; in 1950 there were two, and by 2000 the number of million-cities had increased to 35. According to UN-Habitat (2008), it was anticipated that, by 2010, there would be 22 million-cities spread across seven SADC member-states (Angola, DRC, Madagascar, Mozambique, South Africa, Zambia, Zimbabwe).

Table 4.2 Selected large dams in SADC states

Dam	Capacity (x10⁹m³)	Completion Year
Mutirikwe (Zimbabwe)	1.5	1970
Katse (Lesotho)	2.0	1996
Itezhi-Tezhi (Zambia)	5.0	1978
Gariep (South Africa)	6.0	1972
Cahora Bassa (Mozambique)	52.0	1974
Kariba (Zambia/Zimbabwe)	185.0	1959

Source: SADC (2011: 26).

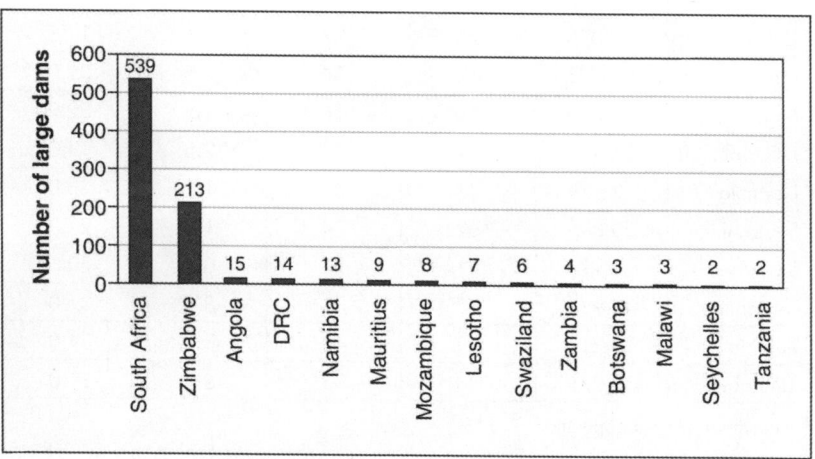

Figure 4.2 Number of large dams (capacity >3 million m³) by SADC country
Source: SADC (2011: 27).

As shown in Table 4.3, SADC populations continue to expand, as does the migration to urban areas, and, in most cases, to the primate city. It is estimated that there are more than 2 million people in Maputo, more than 6.5 million in Luanda, 7 million in Kinshasa, 12.9 million in Johannesburg, 4 million in Dar es Salaam, 1.7 million in Lusaka and 1.5 million in Harare. And while the totals in the capital cities of Botswana, Lesotho and Namibia are much smaller, they constitute significant proportions of their total and urban populations: Gaborone

Table 4.3 Changes in urban population in SADC states

Country	Population (000s)	Per cent population that is urban (1995–99)	Per cent population that is urban (2014)	Per cent population growth (2010–14)	Largest city per cent of total urban population
Angola	22 137	40	43	3.1	55.0
Botswana	2 039	56	57	0.9	9.0*
DRC	69 360	40	42	2.7	38.0
Lesotho	2 098	25	27	1.1	11.8*
Madagascar	23 572	32	34	2.8	31.0
Malawi	16 829	16	16	2.8	32.0
Mozambique	26 473	31	32	2.5	14.0
Namibia	2 179	42	46	1.9	33.0
South Africa	50 895	62	64	1.3	27.0
Swaziland	1 193	21	21	0.9	20.6*
Tanzania	44 973	28	31	3.0	31.0
Zambia	13 216	39	40	3.2	34.0
Zimbabwe	13 076	33	33	3.1	31.0

* Percentage of total population

Source: World Bank Indicators, http://data.worldbank.org/indicator/SP.POP.GROW; http://data.worldbank.org/indicator/SP.URB.TOTL.IN.ZS; http://data.worldbank.org/ indicator/SP.POP.TOTL); UNDP (2014).

231 592, Maseru 178 345 and Windhoek 325 858. Only Malawi, with 16 per cent of its nearly 17 million people, and Swaziland, with 21 per cent of a mere 1.1 million people retain overwhelmingly rural profiles. Mbabane contains only 57 992 and Swaziland's second city of Manzini a mere 25 571. In comparison, taken together, Lilongwe (674 448) and Blantyre (661 256) account for approximately 10 per cent of Malawi's overall population and more than 60 per cent of its total urban population.

One doubts whether even the best-resourced city would have been able to cope with a similar influx of people as that to SADC's capitals. Table 4.4 highlights the abysmal performance in terms of water supply and sanitation across all SADC states, especially in relation to sanitation. Here we see the discrepancies between rural and urban access to improved water sources and overall access to improved forms of sanitation between 2009 and 2012. What should be clear from this table is the shameful performance in the delivery of these basic services to the citizens of SADC states. Given the very generous and broad categorisation of what constitutes 'improved', it is embarrassing in the extreme that despite the concentrated focus on water supply and sanitation in the Millennium Development Goals programme, only Mauritius is able to claim complete coverage. We also know from direct field experience that these figures are inflated as the boreholes being counted in rural areas are often not functioning, and the taps provided in cities have long been vandalised.

In my view, the abiding, severe and in many cases worsening problems with urban water supply and sanitation reflect the underdeveloped nature of SADC states described in Chapter 2. To say that the 'city' is not one thing is to say nothing new – they are complex, organic and ever changing. All cities face challenges of both infrastructure (development of the new, and maintenance and replacement of the old) and access (affordable household-based systems of reticulation, affordable housing, public water and sanitation facilities, and so on). But the SADC's cities contain the complex geographies of 'First World/Fourth World', of the (few) haves living side by side with the (many) have-nots. One may

Table 4.4   SADC state access to improved water and sanitation, rural and urban percentage

State	Access to improved water (2012): Rural	Access to improved water (2012): Urban	Access to improved sanitation (2009)	Access to improved sanitation (2012)
Angola	34	68	56	60
Botswana	93	99	63	64
DRC	29	79	29	31
Lesotho	77	93	28	30
Malawi	83	95	10	10
Mauritius	100	100	90	91
Mozambique	35	80	19	21
Namibia	87	98	31	32
Seychelles	96	96	97	97
South Africa	88	99	72	74
Swaziland	69	94	56	58
Tanzania	44	78	11	12
Zambia	49	85	42	43
Zimbabwe	69	97	40	40

Source: World Bank statistics.

derive a sense of the vast inequalities through statistics, but nothing substitutes for physically navigating one's way across the cityscape. It is no exaggeration to say that few representatives of international financial institutions have ever ventured into high-density spaces. Their concern is with the ways and means of delivering on commitments made by state actors, often at international meetings, not with the particularities of social formation, of who is – to borrow terms from Amartya Sen (1999) – socially included or excluded and why. So, it follows that the 1990s push toward privatisation or corporatisation seemed logical from a distance. It marked a drive for efficiency gains with limited state control. For the masses, long socially excluded, such an approach was tantamount to invoking 'water apartheid'.

Without doubt, the greatest problems of water and sanitation are experienced in the high-density areas of Africa's cities. Originally developed to house a limited number of urban workers, these areas are now densely filled with illegal buildings as add-ons to existing structures, and ringed by even denser squatter/informal settlements. For example, Sakubva is a high-density area built around 1910 to house labourers for the local industries of Mutare, Zimbabwe. At that time, a series of formal housing units (stand-alone two- and three-room houses and one-room row housing) with public standpipes and toilet facilities were built for 3 000 or so people. By 2000 there were more than 50 000 people residing in this area, with all the attendant problems well chronicled throughout the literature on urbanisation in developing countries. In many African cities, the story is the same, but the scale is more dramatic, often by a factor of 10 or 15: built environments designed for 50 000 people, such as Dar es Salaam, now hold an estimated 5 million people. In South Africa, according to the 2011 Census, Soweto, for example, is home to an estimated 1.27 million people, Alexandra township to 798 000, Umlazi township to 404 000, and Khayelitsha to 391 000. Yet water supply and sanitation are not the only challenges. Urban challenges as they relate to water are legion, with the problems of the squatter settlements being but the tip of a complex iceberg. Table 4.5 highlights the interrelationship between historical, structural and personal factors impeding service delivery in the region.

Across the region a debate continues to rage between delivering water with economic efficiency and citizens' rights to water irrespective of cost. This is a political issue, not a water scarcity issue. The South African city has become a battleground of service delivery protests, which are as much about appropriate forms of governance as they are about access to resources. The 2014 special issue of the South African journal *Politikon*, guest edited by Lisa Thompson and entitled 'Reflections on Twenty Years of Democracy from Below', accurately chronicles these struggles. In other SADC states, citizens seem to prefer 'exit' rather than 'voice',

Table 4.5   Challenges and responses in SADC cities

Challenge	Relation to water	Proposed solution	Example
Physical location of the city	Too much/too little, depending on the season; difficult to capture and transport	Large-scale infrastructure development; water demand management; environmental education	Botswana North-South Carrier 2; municipal wastewater reuse in Windhoek; World Bank financed Dar es Salaam water supply and sanitation project; environmental and water education programs in schools across SADC
Segregationist planning in early stages	Limited development of infrastructure; limited extension of services	Continual roll-out through 'phases' of new and revitalised infrastructure, with focus on extension of services to those most in need	Installation of water demand management devices in township areas of Cape Town to ensure both service but also cost recovery
Reactive planning in post-independence era	Disintegrated decision-making; supply-side oriented; donor-driven	IWRM framework; participatory decision-making	Integrated development plans devised across SADC states
Dramatic increase in population	Massive increase in informal housing; ecological degradation	Rehabilitation of resource base (tree planting); decanting and reblocking	Working for Water project in South Africa; removal of invasive species in Namibia; initiation of reblocking of high-density areas in South Africa
Economic crisis of the 1970–80s	Infrastructure decline; self-help	Public-private partnerships (PPPs); micro-enterprise	Dam building across the region; focus on formal small-scale urban enterprise for a variety of services: solid-waste plumbing; informal water markets

Table 4.5 *Continued*

Challenge	Relation to water	Proposed solution	Example
Neoliberal structural adjustment programmes as response to crisis	Privatisation of delivery; user-pay schemes	These are accepted as the de facto way forward, with a recognition that the state must participate in terms of regulation and oversight	Metered standpipes; metered homes with fixed daily limits in South Africa; water kiosks and communal ablution facilities across urban areas
Class/race/caste/tribe/gender divisions	Favouritism and blindness to needs of non-included	Cross-conditionalities from lenders; environmental education	Cap-Net and GWP Southern Africa training on various issues
Poor governance/corruption/patronage/patrimonialism	Continual decline of infrastructure; 'tenderpreneurs'; lack of leadership in a 'social project'	Cross-conditionalities from lenders	Lending based on performance

helping themselves by pirating water supplies for resale to politically marginalised customers. Demand is significant. For example, it is estimated that only 100 000 households have formal, in-house water supply in Dar es Salaam, a city of nearly 5 million people. According to SADC data published in 2012 (SADC, 2012), 61 per cent of the region's 260 million people had access to improved water supply, and only 39 per cent had access to improved forms of sanitation.

In recent years, particularly with the advent of the Millennium Development Goals, a great deal of emphasis has been placed on what is called 'pro-poor urban water and sanitation governance'. What this means is putting the needs of the most vulnerable first when planning systems of delivery for urban water and sanitation. A cursory survey of systems of delivery reveals that those most in need are left to fend for themselves. Lacking political and economic power, the poor are voiceless. Governments often do not know where to begin, particularly when it comes to densely packed squatter settlements. Often times the answer has been to bulldoze their shacks and drive them out of the city, only to see them return again en masse. Providers, too, generally focus on those who are already well served, their ability and willingness to pay being the primary incentive for private and/or public utility attention. Corrupt practices and clientelistic behaviour further erode the will and capacity of local government to deliver services to citizens and residents of the city.

It is a truism to say that access to improved water and sanitation is less about pipes and pumps and more about enabling the poor to help themselves. Put differently, non-resource-specific interventions will go a long way to improving access to the resource itself: better incomes through employment opportunities; the right to land and security of tenure; better information about citizens' rights; and better organised communities able to speak with one voice are all important elements of realising access to improved water and sanitation.

One of the primary impediments to better provision, however, is state-civil society relations. A non-responsive or even repressive state is generally ignored or avoided by the very citizens it is supposed to serve. How to build trust where past practice counsels mutual suspicion is an important question in water for cities. Participatory planning in Cape Town that brings together the City of Cape Town, local NGOs and community groups in the effort to upgrade informal settlements is evidence that there are ways to build trust across the state-civil society divide. However, for every step forward such as the reblocking exercise (see Box 4.1) , there are myriad steps back manifesting as violent social protest in reaction to what people perceive to be non-responsive and dictatorial governments.

Poor governance combined with incompetent public utilities led the rush toward private sector providers, particularly large multinational companies based in the UK, France and elsewhere, throughout the 1990s and into the early 2000s. By and large, this 180-degree turn

> **Box 4.1   Reblocking as Trust Building in Cape Town**
>
> South African cities are unique in that apartheid created 'black spots' on the outskirts of formal urban spaces. The post-apartheid era redrew the boundaries to include these previously formally unacknowledged settled peri-urban spaces. In the intervening 20 years since the end of formal apartheid, millions of people have flooded into the post-apartheid urban space, the majority of whom now occupy 'informal housing', i.e., shacks. South African government policy attempts to 'resettle' these people on 'better land'. This is code for moving them off often valuable urban property into a new hinterland, creating a new sort of spatial apartheid. However, the government, in acknowledging that it cannot meet its commitment to provide formal housing for all, is now committed to shack-upgrading, also known as 'reblocking'. In Cape Town, four settlements have been successfully reblocked: Kuku town, Flamingo Crescent, Sheffield Road and Mtshini Wami. Rather than moving people out, the City is committed to making these spaces safe and serviceable. To achieve these goals, a coalition of local and national NGOs, in league with the City of Cape Town and community groups, have come together in common cause. Is this a viable long-term solution? It is hard to judge, when the needs are so pressing in the short term. In my view, however, this is a necessary start if we are ever to bring the state and civil society closer together in a common social project.
>
> *See Tshabalala and Mxobo (2014).*

from public to private was an unmitigated disaster. Rare is the example where a private sector provider followed the terms as agreed to in their contract. For most of the last 10 years, the donor world has been crab-walking away from the private sector toward a middle ground where it is recognised that only oversight and regulation by a competent state authority will be able to ensure a provider's delivery on contract.

For a while these public-private partnerships – or PPPs, as they are popularly known – were regarded as the best way forward with, in my view, a mostly positive example to be found in both Rand Water, as the bulk provider to major municipalities such as Johannesburg in

South Africa, and Johannesburg Water, as an independent company with the City of Johannesburg as its sole shareholder, as the provider of water to consumers in the municipality. Johannesburg Water further subcontracts many of its activities to private companies. There are several reasons to consider this a relative success:

- Apartheid planning attempted to keep the races separate. The black townships of Alexandra, in the heart of what was meant to be all-white Johannesburg, and Soweto, located 27 kilometres from the Central Business District (CBD), shows how this planning failed miserably. The 'separateness' in this case emerged in the limited services provided to these densely populated areas. In the post-apartheid context, this First World/Fourth World urban conglomeration has been roped together as the City of Johannesburg Metropolitan Municipality. Given the scale of the demands for water and sanitation across the Johannesburg metropolitan area, the fact that it has been not only able to deliver but to upgrade and extend services is commendable.
- The water delivered to households is potable, meaning that it is safe to drink, with Johannesburg Water having achieved and maintained its platinum Blue Drop rating from the Department of Water Affairs, with the latest (2014) evaluation seeing it achieve a 96.06 per cent score.
- The City's Green Drop silver rating (measuring monitoring, microbiological, physical and chemical characteristics) for wastewater management is considerably lower, but also much better than almost all municipalities across South Africa.
- Johannesburg Water is responsible for the operation and maintenance of 10 957.88 kilometres of distribution pipes for potable water, 33 water towers, and 87 reservoirs and pumping stations. In terms of wastewater management, it is responsible for six wastewater treatment plants (handling 950 megalitres/day), 38 pumping stations and 10 058.03 kilometres of sewerage pipes. It maintains a transparent

system of record keeping and reporting, and reaches out to the public via various forms of telecommunications and social media.

One should not underestimate the positive achievement of maintenance and extension of delivery through this corporatised entity. This claim is not meant to distract the reader from the intense battles being fought over access, the appropriate means of access, questions of cost recovery and the role of civil society in decision-making. In addition, there are many remaining problems, inherited from a combination of Western modelling and apartheid engineering, and currently exacerbated in the context of a prolonged El Niño-driven drought. Compared to many other utilities in the region, however, Johannesburg Water is, in my view, an organisation worth emulating.

Increasingly, municipalities have realised that PPPs are not enough, and that communities must also be directly involved through, for example, civil society organisations. Hence we now have the unwieldy acronym PPCPs – public-private community partnerships. In highly unequal societies, such as Botswana, Namibia, Zimbabwe and South Africa, with Gini coefficients of income inequality nearing 0.7, differential service is regarded by the poor as a continuation of neglect and disrespect. The introduction of water kiosks, prepaid meters and flow-restriction devices that kick in when users fail to pay are highly contentious. Sometimes, even with community involvement, it is not possible to achieve buy-in regarding the possibilities for expansion and delivery.

While there are many issues related to under-performing utilities, it seems clear that the state (through goal setting, subsidies, incentives and regulation) and the market (through responsiveness to consumer needs) have roles to play in ensuring that the provider or providers – be it a public or private entity – has enough incentive to deliver as per the terms of their contract. It is a delicate balancing act. When it goes wrong, it goes very wrong indeed, as the so-called 'water wars' in Cochabamba, Bolivia, showed. Given the variability of settlement patterns, particularly in the primate cities of the global South, whether expansion will mean networked or non-networked systems, prepaid meters with automatic shut-off points (or not), step-wise tariff structures, and adherence to global standards that may be beyond the technical and financial ability of the city, are all issues that require an open conversation. History shows that where non-transparent decisions have been taken 'on behalf of' the poor, even where a desire to help is the true motivator, there will be problems. The recent so-called 'toilet wars' in Cape Town, South Africa, are an excellent example. Paternalism worldwide is generally greeted with stubborn disobedience.

What is very clear is that people need and deserve respect. Where the poor are consulted and made partners in problem solving, the innovations are as remarkable as the results. A 2011 special issue of the *Journal of Enterprising Communities*, guest edited by Kevin McKague and colleagues, highlights the numerous possibilities for success – from water supply and sanitation systems, to community-led access to household supplies of energy. Where people are treated as either undisciplined children or a problem to be contained or both, whatever the state attempts to do on their behalf will be met with contempt. As in the South African case, sanitation needs notwithstanding, toilets will fly when citizens feel that they have been disrespected.

Rural water supply

Rural areas are forgotten lands populated by forgotten people, until, of course, they are not. In a democracy, rural people matter at voting time. It is then that you see the politicians traipsing through the fields or walking along the dusty streets of cow towns while making promises of every sort, leaving behind a few bags of fertiliser and seed. All politicians promise water. Left to fend for themselves, or minimally serviced through a minor government ministry, as technology advances rural people find themselves at the centre of developmental struggles. Their lands, usually managed under a common property regime, are regazetted and reapportioned to the wealthy who are able to purchase them as freehold lands under policies of privatisation. Or their lands are flooded out and the people themselves made to move as new dams are built to service government-supported irrigation schemes for commercial agriculture. Or their drylands are coveted by industry hungry for the minerals to be mined from their depths. So, out of sight, out of mind; but, once in sight, generally a problem. And when in sight, the end result is often that whatever water you had gets taken away.

What to do about rural centres, such as Kitwe, in central Zambia, or Mzuzu in north-central Malawi, or Maun, in northwestern Botswana? Far from the centres of power, small towns are notoriously under-serviced, with government-supported centralised systems of supply delivering water erratically, often expensively, and usually of irregular quality. Sanitation systems are even worse: while it is easy to sink a borehole, dealing with liquid and solid waste is more complex. It is estimated that across the global South, some 90 per cent of cities dump their raw sewerage directly into water bodies. When you live upland, as in Dedza or Zomba in Malawi, your waste becomes someone else's problem. But when you live in a coastal town, such as Beira on the Indian Ocean or Musoma on the Tanzanian side of Lake Victoria, your waste becomes the cause of many of your own health problems.

Two significant problems relating to water for rural people are geographical location and population density. Rural settlements are often in remote areas with small populations, often home to fewer than 500 people. Governments generally set thresholds for the delivery of services, attempting to entice people to cluster together in what are called 'growth points': more than 500 people, then you will get a government-supported borehole and health clinic; more than 1 500 and you may get a school as well. According to a 2013 UN-Habitat report, the adequacy of service is a function of proximity, scale and numbers: if people live near to each other in significant numbers there will emerge a local economy that will bolster people's ability to pay for improved services while also lowering the unit costs of delivery on the part of the provider.

Where people refuse to move, then they will be left to fend for themselves, collecting water from rivers and streams, hand-digging wells, or travelling great distances to collect piped water. Water services, therefore, often fall to international NGOs such as WaterAid or Engineers Without Borders, who will drill a well and claim a photo opportunity. A bit cynical, perhaps, but such activities often reproduce and reinforce a wide variety of problems and social pathologies: for instance, in a North-South context, that people of colour need 'Western' help because they do not know how to help themselves; and in a state-civil society context, where NGOs are active without involving local government or acting against local government's own policies, the trust and social capital necessary to enhance not only people's lives but their lives as citizens with rights and the practice of governments with responsibilities is never built.

Rural water supply in Ngamiland, Botswana

Let us now turn to a case study of rural water supply in Ngamiland, Botswana, where I lived and worked for four years during the first decade of the twenty-first century and continue to return to. Ngamiland district occupies the northwestern part of Botswana, covering an area of approximately 109 000 km². Maun is Ngamiland's district headquarters, its largest settlement with a population of some 44 000 and a planning area of 446 km². There are 124 000 people in the district, 70 per cent of whom live within 10 kilometres of the Okavango River main channel. The Okavango is a 'linear oasis', running through an otherwise arid environment, and the livelihoods of the people are dependent on access to it. The majority of settlements are clustered along the edges of the delta and panhandle, and Maun – despite its status as the administrative centre – is a town with widely scattered settlements. The Thamalakane is the primary outflow river from the delta and the town is settled primarily along one side of it.

Access to water means more than just drinking water or household water for people in Ngamiland: fishing, transportation, a source of reeds for making thatch. Water is central to livelihoods in rural areas around the world. In this part of rural Africa, humans and livestock must compete with wildlife for the resource. This means that having to draw water from rivers, or to wash your clothes at the shores of these waters, is often very dangerous business particularly for women, whose tasks in traditional societies these tend to be. Research shows that women and children fall prey to crocodiles across the region during the course of their domestic chores.

In statistical (see the tables earlier) and practical terms, Botswana has performed very well in terms of facilitating people's access to household water. Like many other countries, however, they have not done so well in terms of access to improved forms of sanitation. Ngamiland presents a particularly difficult setting for realising water and sanitation goals. People are scattered far and wide in tiny settlements, with only Maun having a significant concentration of people.

How a government defines your settlement matters a great deal: having fewer than 500 people suggests to government that you do not have the requisite economic potential and employment generation capacity to merit more than a borehole or two. For the 478 settlements with fewer than 250 residents in this region, this means that they will be left largely to fend for themselves. In law, government establishes particular standards for supplying water. But in practice, once supplied twice forgotten. District councils and municipalities are well known for being the weakest links in the governance chain: though closest to the people, they lack human, financial and technical capacity. Regular service, then, will usually mean that those responsible for maintaining your supply will only show up once you have made your way to the head office to complain in person.

According to data compiled by researchers at the Okavango Research Institute (Kujinga et al. 2014a; Kujinga et al. 2014b), approximately 33 per cent of residents in Ngamiland West and 11 per cent in Ngamiland East have access to water on their own plots of land. What this data also shows is that a good number of households depend for their water on unimproved sources: dams, pans, rivers, springs. To assume that water resources are more readily available or of higher quality in Maun than elsewhere in Ngamiland is to assume too much. The town is served by two well-fields, located some distance from the town centre. Water is pumped to the town via several diesel-powered engines. People surveyed in the town revealed that water supply is erratic, expensive, unreliable and delivers a resource of questionable quality. Ungazetted settlements, as one would expect, are worse, particularly as people here must compete with wildlife for access to the resource.

When presented with these findings, government officials' two most common responses were: there is nothing we can do; and people must leave their remote areas and move to town where services are better. This is in fact government policy – to encourage people to shift to larger settlement areas. One problem with this, however, is government's failure to understand that household water is only one small aspect of rural people's relationship to water and the land.

In summarising government's perspective on the difficulties in supplying water to rural areas, one can see emerge a pattern common to rural areas almost everywhere. Save for the odd regional peculiarity, poor service is generally a function of limited human, financial and technical resources on the part of government, and limited economic and political power on the part of the vast majority of rural people. The same sorts of issues arise when one raises concerns regarding water quality.

The pursuit of 'productive water', on the other hand, at once recreates socio-economic inequalities (for example, by encouraging people to drill their own boreholes, those most likely to drill are wealthy individuals) and has the opposite effect of that intended (rather than relieve pressure around the delta itself, it creates pressure on groundwater resources through, for example, the indiscriminate drilling of wells that end up depleting the groundwater resource).

The picture that emerges is one of a sort of Wild West, to paraphrase a popular Hollywood characterisation of the nineteenth-century American frontier. Self-help is the order of the day. Sure, the state will supply as per the legal system, but beyond the initial construction of facilities, rural areas are so poorly funded that operation and maintenance problems quickly arise and persist, so leading to the constant complaint that 'government never does anything for us'. Thus there is a disjuncture between policy and practice: on one hand, official government policy is to provide in-house plumbing to everyone, but on the other hand, data reveals a significant shortfall in delivery.

Conclusion

It should be clear from this chapter that while the laws and policies look good, performance on the ground is lacking. There are an endless series of problems related to domestic water. As shown here, delivery of small water, irrespective of the quality, is a significant social problem. What then is to be done? In the South African context, the answer seems to be to engage with the state, to demand one's rights as articulated in the Constitution, to take to the streets and to protest when necessary. This gives me hope. But across the rest of the SADC region, the dual economy reinforces dual societies: people seem relatively satisfied to go their own way. In my view, this is a recipe for disaster. With the potential of climate change to alter hydrological cycles, 'self-help' may no longer suffice – if, in looking at poverty levels across the region, it ever did. Engagement is necessary. If the water wars of southern Africa are primarily intra-state conflicts over small water, what then of the nation-state in a transboundary setting? Chapter 5 turns to examine how, in contrast to the evidence provided in this chapter, SADC policy-makers paradoxically seem eminently capable of sharing transnational water, while remaining wholly incapable of equitably serving the citizens of their own states.

5

Sharing Water
Transboundary Waters in the SADC

As highlighted in Chapters 1 and 2, water falls and flows, while states occupy fixed space. The organisation of the region's states stands at odds with the character of its water resource flows, both in space and in time. If people and ecosystems are to survive and thrive, this natural resource must be managed holistically – in other words, in terms of the hydrological cycle, because that cycle changes over time. As shown in Chapters 3 and 4, the historical approach to water management is the capturing and taming of a fugitive and wild resource – note the language of discipline and control. Where the resource is shared by two or more sovereign states, however, resource capture – physically through the application of various infrastructure and legally through the codification of actions in policy and law – is bound to be problematic: socially, politically, economically, environmentally and possibly militarily. For many years there has been speculation regarding the possibility of water wars in the region, with several basins having been identified to be 'at risk' of violent conflict. Hence the importance of sharing water fairly and sustainably. The focus of this chapter, then, is on the process and practice of sharing the region's water by SADC member states.

Conceptualising co-operation
In his important 2006 study, Ken Conca argues that the goal of global water governance is to embed these often contentious and conflict-ridden interests and needs within 'institutional configurations and orientations'. In other words, to create an institutional structure and process for dealing with multiple interests regarding a shared resource

so as to minimise negative outcomes and to maximise shared benefits. Conca describes the common pathway in relation to territory, authority and knowledge: the sovereign state is the territorial reference point for water governance and management; the state (as represented by its government) is the acknowledged authority for decisions regarding access, use and management of water resources; decisions regarding access, use and management derive from expert/specialist knowledge deployed by the state in service of the national interest. As shown in Steve Solomon's magisterial 2010 study, such an approach to water governance and management has been common throughout the ages, especially during the high-modern/industrial period where states, generally in competition with each other, engaged in a concerted 'hydraulic mission' to capture water resources in the interests of political and economic power. This tendency to govern and manage a fugitive resource in terms of the needs of a spatially static state, a shared resource in terms of partial, 'national' interests (as determined by elites), and a resource essential to the functioning of a complex system in terms of highly specific expert knowledge designed to put a river 'to work', is now widely regarded as the source of environmentally unsustainable, socially inequitable and economically inefficient 'maldevelopment'.

In direct response to the perceived negative cycle of unsustainability set in motion by embedded practices, IWRM alongside good governance emerged as the twin meta-norms shaping the way water resource governance and management should be organised. To achieve the 'triple-E common good' – i.e., environmental sustainability, economic efficiency and social equity – common frameworks, conceptualisations and practices as they pertain to territory, authority and knowledge must change:

- the appropriate territorial space must be the river basin;
- the appropriate governing/managing authority must be the relevant stakeholder group (which would include the state as only one, albeit centrally important, actor); and
- decisions regarding resource access, use and management must be taken on the basis of inclusive forms of knowledge

derived from stakeholders (e.g., indigenous knowledge and/
or so-called 'citizen science'), wherein 'expert science' would
constitute only one part of the knowledge tree.

This perspective constitutes the high-water mark in a more than four-decade flow of knowledge between and among a wide array of policy-makers, practitioners and stakeholders. In 1972, the United Nations Conference on the Human Environment was held in Stockholm, Sweden. Among many other things, the meeting gave birth to two very important initiatives: the United Nations Environment Program (UNEP), housed in Nairobi, Kenya; and a cascading series of global activities examining the state of the world's freshwater resources – e.g., the Mar del Plata UN Water Conference in 1977; the UN Water and Sanitation Decade launched in 1981; the UN International Decade for Action: 'Water for Life' 2005–2015; and so on up to the Seventh World Water Forum held in Korea in April 2015. From the inception of these activities two primary debates have ensued: the first is about whether our freshwater glass is half full or half empty. As discussed in Chapter 3, much of the argument turns on the interrelationship between a 'finite' resource – i.e., freshwater which is said to comprise a mere 0.0007 per cent of all water on the earth – and a rapidly growing global population. In many ways, this debate divides developed countries – that see the glass half empty and argue for demand-side interventions – from developing countries, particularly China and India, who see the glass half full and argue for supply-side augmentation. The second debate is about the ways and means to ensure provision of water in appropriate quantities and qualities for all human and environmental needs. The answer to this question depends on (1) your position in the first debate; and (2) whether you see water as an economic good, where access/provision is a function of both demand and ability to pay, or as a social/public good, where the state must provide access because the right to water is a basic human right.

The character and content of these debates, as well as the policies and practices that have followed, were fundamentally shaped by two international meetings held in 1992: the International Conference on Water and the Environment, held in Dublin, Ireland, in January; and the UN Conference on the Environment and Development, also known as 'the Earth Summit', held in Rio de Janeiro, Brazil, in June. The former gave rise to the Dublin Principles; the latter to Agenda 21.

As shown in Box 5.1, the Dublin Principles revolve around the ideas that water is scarce, that it should be managed collectively, that women play a vital role, and that it should be treated as an economic good. Chapter 18 of Agenda 21 is devoted to the Protection and Quality of Supply of Freshwater Resources, lays out an action agenda with financial estimates attached, describes water as an economic and a social good, places a strong emphasis on environmental sustainability and, most importantly, articulates the concept of Integrated Water Resources Management (IWRM). Thus, these two meetings, while emerging out of numerous previous forums, formally shaped the agenda for debate, discussion and practice of the global governance of freshwater resources for the ensuing two decades. But trying to shape the global water governance and management agenda in terms of the way things 'should be' immediately opened a Pandora's Box of problems and challenges, almost all of which stem from present beneficiaries' perceptions regarding anticipated future losses to be incurred through the new institutional configurations and orientations. Put simply: water is power, and to revise and rearticulate water institutions is to challenge existing forms and bases of power. Moreover, to shape the debate about better governance within the context of 'a scarce resource' could only have resulted in reactive responses to hold on to what you have. Put differently, 'scarcity' closed off rather than opened up avenues for new thinking about water governance and management. So, in response to the hopefulness of the new governance and management thinking, there came a deluge of resistance, marked in part by concerted attempts to capture and shape agendas. Aside from rafts of research paper, progress toward good water governance was halting at best.

Partly in response to the slow pace of progress, at the second World Water Forum held in The Hague in 2000, the Netherlands' King

Box 5.1   The Dublin Principles

Principle No. 1 – Fresh water is a finite and vulnerable resource, essential to sustain life, development and the environment

Since water sustains life, effective management of water resources demands a holistic approach, linking social and economic development with protection of natural ecosystems. Effective management links land and water uses across the whole of a catchment area or groundwater aquifer.

Principle No. 2 – Water development and management should be based on a participatory approach, involving users, planners and policy-makers at all levels

The participatory approach involves raising awareness of the importance of water among policy-makers and the general public. It means that decisions are taken at the lowest appropriate level, with full public consultation and involvement of users in the planning and implementation of water projects.

Principle No. 3 – Women play a central part in the provision, management and safeguarding of water

This pivotal role of women as providers and users of water and guardians of the living environment has seldom been reflected in institutional arrangements for the development and management of water resources. Acceptance and implementation of this principle requires positive policies to address women's specific needs and to equip and empower women to participate at all levels in water resources programmes, including decision-making and implementation, in ways defined by them.

Principle No. 4 – Water has an economic value in all its competing uses and should be recognised as an economic good.

Within this principle, it is vital to recognise first the basic right of all human beings to have access to clean water and sanitation at an affordable price. Past failure to recognise the economic value of water has led to wasteful and environmentally damaging uses of the resource. Managing water as an economic good is an important way of achieving efficient and quitable use, and of encouraging conservation and protection of water resources.

Source: https://www.wmo.int/pages/prog/hwrp/documents/english/icwedece.html.

Willem-Alexander, at the time Prince of Orange, declared that the world water crisis was 'a crisis of governance'. Scholars and development practitioners rallied around this phrase, further arguing that there was, in fact, no 'water crisis' at all, but a 'crisis of water management'. Thus there came to be a heavy emphasis on the political and managerial aspects of water problems and challenges, while – in line with the global economic focus on neoliberalism – also a strong emphasis on the need for markets and private sector actors in infrastructure development for water supply and sanitation.

The logic informing IWRM seems impeccable: the problems with water derive from fragmentation across government sectors, divisive approaches and understandings of the resource across the watershed, and narrow understandings of what water is (i.e., blue) and for (i.e., humans and (agri)industry). Nevertheless, while most water professionals were in agreement on the problems with management, means of addressing the issue were less clear and more contentious. Approaches to good water governance were also fraught with argument, with actors such as the World Bank and the World Water Council taking a 'checklist' approach to governance that looked suspiciously like standard definitions of corporate governance. At the same time, a strong leftist critique emerged, challenging what was perceived to be the extension of the neoliberal agenda, complete with political and economic cross-conditionalities, to the water sector. Such an approach, in their critical view, only served to facilitate improvement and extension of services to the empowered and further marginalisation of those most in need of even the barest daily minimum. For many on the left, guaranteeing a human right to water became the objective point of departure for appropriate governance and management of water resources.

While masking a great deal of complexity within and between these issues, these broad brush strokes nevertheless adequately characterise the general trends in approaches to the global governance of water. Because water is not an ordinary good, a diverse array of stakeholders with a diverse array of needs and interests are ineluctably drawn together to discuss how best to allocate this shared resource, while an equally diverse array are often left out of 'formal' discussions.

Institutionalisation in SADC

In the nearly 25 years since the creation of the Dublin Principles, the SADC states have written and revised national water resource strategies, and reshaped their water laws, policies and procedures to be in line with these emergent global norms. Pan-African (e.g., the African Union (AU), African Ministerial Council on Water (AMCOW)) and regional (e.g., SADC, COMESA, ECOWAS, IGAD) organisations function as discursive nodal points whereby member states, globally (e.g., World Bank, Global Water Partnership) and regionally (e.g., African Development Bank (AfDB), Development Bank of Southern Africa (DBSA)) influential actors, along with donor states (e.g., DfID, GIZ, EU, USAID), private companies and (international) non-governmental organisations hammer out the particularities of turning policy into practice.

The diffusion of emerging global norms into the SADC region was enabled by complementary regional actors, forces and factors. For example, one can point to the near-simultaneous advent of several interrelated factors that served to push the region's decision-makers in a new direction:

- the formal end of apartheid in South Africa and the Nelson Mandela-led 'new' South Africa becoming 'part of' the SADCC region, rather than 'apart from' it;
- widespread multi-year drought across the region from the late-1980s to the mid-1990s;
- South Africa's desire to fit into the world and become a good global citizen after apartheid;
- the rise of the 'basin approach' to water management fitting well with a SADC strategy of regional integration;
- donor state interest in the peacemaking potential of regional resource use co-operation; and
- national goals for sustainable economic development and poverty alleviation.

Shared water

According to Conca (2006), a key entry point for institution-building in defence of the world's river basins is the fact that most of the world's biggest rivers cross national borders. It is estimated that there are at least 263 international river basins, with some estimates suggesting more than 300. According to AMCOW 2012 data, shared river basins in Africa account for 61 per cent of the continent, 77 per cent of the population, and over 90 per cent of the total available water. There are 15 shared river basins in the SADC.

Legal foundation: The Protocol

SADC leaders reacted positively to these pressures and opportunities through the creation of the regional water protocol (signed in 1995 and acceded to in 1998). With the 1997 creation of the United Nations Convention on the Law of Non-Navigational Uses of International Watercourses (UNC), which was ratified into law in 2014, the 1995 protocol was revised in 2000 and ultimately adopted in 2003. Based on Article 22 of the SADC Treaty, and viewed as 'a vehicle for regional integration', the spirit and intent of the Protocol is to collectively manage the region's shared water resources for sustainable economic and social development of all SADC citizens. Specifically, the objective of the Protocol as specified in Article 2 is 'to foster closer co-operation for judicious, sustainable and co-ordinated management, protection and utilisation of shared watercourses and advance the SADC agenda for regional integration'. The background to the Protocol has been studied extensively. The Protocol is meant to inform the actions of all member states with regard to water resources policy, law and management at national level. At the same time, it underpins a wide variety of inter-state actions, particularly in the context of developing transboundary river basins and their management, including the setting up of relevant basin institutions.

Given that 70 per cent of the region's land falls within an international river basin, and the centrality of water in economic development, the

Table 5.1   International river basins in SADC

Basin name and catchment area	Basin states	Special features
Buzi 31 000 km²	Mozambique, Zimbabwe	Mean annual runoff 2 500 MCM/year Joint Water Commission between Mozambique and Zimbabwe to address issues related to transboundary watercourses, including the Pungwe, Buzi and Save river basins – 2002
Kunene/Cunene 106 500 km²	Angola, Namibia	Mean annual runoff 5 500 MCM/year Third Water Use Agreement – 1969 (between South Africa and Portugal) – 1990 (between Angola and Namibia) Cunene Permanent Joint Technical Commission (PJTC) – 2006
Cuvelai 100 000 km²	Angola, Namibia	Mean annual runoff 130 MCM/year (at the ephemeral, endoreic Etosha pan) No agreement but receives waters from the Kunene
Incomati/Komati 50 000 km²	Mozambique, South Africa, Swaziland	Mean annual runoff 3 500 MCM/year Komati Basin Water Authority (SA and Swaziland – Driekoppies and Maguga dams) – 1993 Tripartite Interim Agreement on the Incomati and Maputo Watercourses (Inco-Maputo Tripartite Permanent Technical Committee) – 2002
Limpopo 415 000 km²	Botswana, Mozambique, South Africa, Zimbabwe	Mean annual runoff 5 500 MCM/year LBPTC – 1986 LIMCOM – 2003
Maputo/Pongola 32 000 km²	Mozambique, South Africa, Swaziland	Mean annual runoff 2 500 MCM/year Inco-Maputo Tripartite Permanent Technical Committee – 2002
Nata Karoo sub-basin	Botswana, Zimbabwe	Mostly ephemeral and considered to be of little international importance though climate change may alter this
Okavango 530 000 km²	Angola, Botswana, Namibia	Mean annual runoff 10 000 MCM/year (at the 'panhandle' of the Okavango Delta) Permanent OKACOM – 1994

Table 5.1 *Continued*

Basin name and catchment area	Basin states	Special features
Orange-Senqu 850 000 km²	Botswana, Lesotho, Namibia, South Africa	Mean annual runoff 10 000 MCM/year ORASECOM – 2000 Trans-Caledon Tunnel Authority (Lesotho, South Africa: Lesotho Highlands Water Project) – 1986
Pungwe 32 500 km²	Mozambique, Zimbabwe	Mean annual runoff 3 000 MCM/year Joint Water Commission between Mozambique and Zimbabwe to address issues related to transboundary watercourses including the Pungwe, Buzi and Save river basins – 2002
Rovuma 155 500 km²	Malawi, Mozambique, Tanzania	Mean annual runoff 15 000 MCM/year Rovuma Joint Watercourse Commission (Mozambique/Tanzania) – 2006
Save 92 500 km²	Mozambique, Zimbabwe	Mean annual runoff 7 000 MCM/year Joint Water Commission between Mozambique and Zimbabwe to address issues related to transboundary watercourses including the Pungwe, Buzi and Save river basins – 2002
Umbeluzi 10 900 km²	Mozambique, Swaziland	Mean annual runoff 600 MCM/year Joint Permanent Technical Water Commission – n.d.
Zaire/Congo 3 800 000 km²	Angola, Democratic Republic of Congo, Republic of Congo, Central African Republic, Cameroon, Tanzania, Zambia	Mean annual runoff 1 260 000 MCM/year International Commission of the Congo-Oubangui-Sangha – 1999 (came into force 2003) (Cameroon, CAR, DRC, Congo) Lake Tanganyika Authority (Burundi-DRC-Tanzania-Zambia) – 2008
Zambezi 1 400 000 km²	Angola, Botswana, Malawi, Namibia, Mozambique, Tanzania, Zambia, Zimbabwe	Mean annual runoff 94 000 MCM/year Zambezi River Authority (Zambia, Zimbabwe Kariba Dam) – 1987 ZAMCOM Agreement – 2004 (ratified 2011)

MCM = million cubic metres

Source: adapted (and corrected) from Swatuk (2002); original based on Ohlsson (1995). Heyns (2003); LIMCOM, ORASECOM, SADC websites.

revised SADC Protocol on Shared Watercourses is a seminal document in international water co-operation. According to one long-time regional water professional, the Protocol grew out of riparian states' inability to move forward on a Zambezi River agreement in 1993, at which point it was decided to pursue a regional agreement instead. The revised Protocol takes into account the 1966 Helsinki Rules and the UNC. The 1966 Helsinki Rules by the International Law Association (ILA) most notably established the principle of a state's right to a 'reasonable and equitable share in the beneficial use of the waters of an international drainage basin'.

The UNC is a framework convention, therefore enabling flexibility for basin states to 'enter into agreements . . . which apply and adjust the provisions of the present Convention to the characteristics and uses of a particular watercourse or part thereof' as contained in Article 3(3). Article 2 defines a watercourse as 'a system of surface and groundwater constituting by virtue of their physical relationship a unitary whole and normally flowing into a common terminus.'

The Convention lays out general principles for the content of basin-specific agreements, some of which are as follows:

- Article 5: Calls for states to adhere to the principle of 'equitable and reasonable use' of international watercourses within their territories.
- Article 7: Obligates states to 'prevent the causing of significant harm' to other watercourse states in their use of a shared watercourse.
- Article 8: Obligates states to co-operate on basis of sovereign equality, territorial integrity, mutual benefits, good faith and to consider establishing joint management mechanisms or commissions to facilitate co-operation.
- Article 9: Calls for the regular exchange of information and data.
- Article 11: Requires states to exchange information and consult with other states on any planned activity.

- Article 12: Requires prior notification of any planned measure 'which may have a significant adverse effect' on other watercourse states.
- Articles 20–23: Deal with environmental concerns such as ecosystem preservation, pollution control, control of alien species, and protection and preservation of the marine environment.
- Article 33: Lays out dispute resolution procedures, including an obligation to 'peacefully' resolve disputes; endorse the use of arbitration and mediation and develop procedures for the creation of fact-finding missions.

Importantly, in defining a watercourse in terms of 'hydrological reality' – as opposed to simply surface waters – and by including the principle of 'prevention of significant harm', this UN Convention moved a step closer to managing water within its natural, holistic setting, although it continued to focus on the right of states to determine activities, and on the watercourse itself rather than the wider basin.

In light of these provisions, the SADC Revised Water Protocol specifically seeks to:

- promote and facilitate the establishment of shared watercourse agreements and Shared Watercourse Institutions for the management of shared watercourses;
- advance the sustainable, equitable and reasonable utilisation of the shared watercourses;
- promote a co-ordinated and integrated environmentally sound development and management of shared watercourses;
- promote the harmonisation and monitoring of legislation and policies for planning, development, conservation, protection of shared watercourses, and allocation of the resources thereof; and
- promote research and technology development, information exchange, capacity-building, and the application of appropriate technologies in shared watercourses management.

Included in the Protocol are key aspects such as:

- SADC Tribunal: 'A Tribunal shall be constituted to ensure adherence to and to ensure the proper interpretation of the provisions of this Treaty and subsidiary instruments and to adjudicate upon such disputes as may be referred to it. Decisions of this Tribunal shall be final and binding.'
- Article 2b: Advance the sustainable, equitable and reasonable utilisation of the shared watercourses; promote co-ordinated and integrated environmentally sound development and management of shared waters.
- Article 4 outlines a number of important specific provisions:
  - 4.1a and b focus on the need to provide information and notification of any planned measures;
  - 4.1g(ii) The consultations and negotiations shall be conducted on the basis that each state must in good faith pay reasonable regard to the rights and legitimate interests of other states;
  - 4.2 concerns environmental protection and preservation and highlights ecosystems, pollution, alien species, and aquatic environments, to name several; and
  - 4.3 discusses management in terms of such things as flow, construction of regulation works and describes the need for prevention and mitigation of harmful conditions due to natural or human causes. It also describes the need for co-ordinated waste management.
- Article 5 sets forth the Institutional Framework for regional water resources governance. Article 5.3 focuses on Shared Watercourse Institutions and makes provision for the following:
  - 5.3a Watercourse states undertake to establish appropriate institutions such as watercourse commissions, water authorities or boards as may be determined;
  - 5.3b The responsibilities of such institutions shall be determined by the nature of their objectives, which

must be in conformity with the principles set out in this protocol; and

- 5.3c Shared watercourse institutions shall provide on a regular basis or as required by the Water Sector Co-ordinating Unit all the information necessary to assess progress on the implementation of this Protocol, including the development of their respective agreements.

To be sure, the agreement is not perfect. For example, Article 6.1 makes special note that prior activities are not subject to the agreement, so removing any controversial hydraulic works from the purview of the SADC Water Division. Due to governance issues in Zimbabwe, the Tribunal was, for a time, moribund, only being revived in 2012 through a separate SADC Protocol on the Tribunal and Rules and Procedures. Nevertheless, the Protocol provides a firm base for regional actors to treat water as a regional public good whose management should be to the benefit of all. Inevitably, disputes will arise. Article 7 deals with Settlement of Disputes and states that SADC states shall strive to resolve disputes amicably (7.1). Any disputes not settled amicably shall be referred to the Tribunal (7.2); and where SADC decides to take action against a member state, that state can ask for 'an advisory opinion' (7.3).

Relevance of the Protocol for good water governance and management
In canvassing regional water professionals regarding their opinions on the relevance of the Protocol to sharing regional waters sustainably, equitably and efficiently (the IWRM triple-Es), criticisms emerged in three issue areas: the primacy of sovereignty as an impediment to true regional co-operation; the need for more deeply realised 'regional community' before regional water sharing could be made more meaningful; and the weakness of the Protocol due to its highly generalised form.

At the same time, support for the Protocol is widespread, particularly in the important areas of legal-institutional frameworks and functional practices.

Legal-institutional

According to one river basin official who was interviewed by the author and wished to remain anonymous, it is better to have a written document – however unsatisfactory it may be – than to have no document at all. For many of the region's water professionals, the Protocol's main importance is its role in forming the legal basis for the drafting of transboundary basin agreements, and for guiding state behaviour on particular shared river basins. In his words:

> The Protocol establishes the guidelines, founded in international water law principles, for good conduct and co-operation to manage transboundary water sources and to study the potential of the rivers (hydropower, water supply, irrigation, fishing, navigation, etc.) long before conflicts arise. These studies are done jointly, it develops mutual trust, understanding and the facts are agreed upon as we go along. In this way the expectations and fears of the up and downstream basin states are discussed while the situation is still amicable and not by the time conflict situations arise.

The Protocol is argued to form the basis for the harmonisation of water and related resource policy and law both at the regional scale and on specific rivers. It is the most relevant in ensuring regional harmonisation as far as the management of shared basins is concerned. Article 6(3) of the Protocol stipulates that watercourse states may enter into watercourse-specific agreements, but such agreements must apply the provisions of the Protocol to the watercourse in question.

In the absence of specific inter-state agreements, or functioning river basin organisations, the Protocol is said to have provided the means for such positive outcomes as the Inco-Maputo Interim Agreement and the recent joint completion of a benefit-sharing study on the Zambezi.

According to one long-time participant in issues related to regional water governance:

On the Incomati, South Africa is under immense pressure to deliver the agreed-upon minimum cross-border flow at Komatipoort, as enshrined in the Interim Inco-Maputo Agreement concluded in 2002; it cannot be proven that that agreement would not have existed without the Revised Protocol, but I like to believe that it was an important contextual factor.

According to a senior water manager, the Protocol is mostly used by the region's River Basin Organisations (RBOs) and Commissions (e.g., on the Okavango (OKACOM), Orange-Senqu (ORASECOM), Limpopo (LIMCOM), and the Zambezi (ZAMCOM)) and it is the presence of the protocol that makes RBO agreements possible.

Functionalism
Classic regional integration theory, as articulated in the 1960s and 1970s by scholars such as Oran Young (1969), and Robert Keohane and Joseph Nye (1977), concentrated heavily on functionalism, believing that co-operation in one area would spill over into other areas, so building 'peace in parts'. For Namibian scholar André du Pisani (2001), while the creation of SADCC out of the 1980 Lusaka Declaration was more of a political exercise than it was an economic endeavour, at least three of the organisation's four founding principles continue to resound across present-day SADC:

- forging links to create a genuine and equitable regional organization;
- mobilising resources to promote the implementation of national, inter-state and regional policies; and
- acting in a concerted fashion so as to secure international co-operation within the framework of SADCC's strategy of economic liberation.

Indeed, with regard to the continued place of politics in regional relations, a senior SADC bureaucrat stated:

Currently, although negotiations in the Zambezi Basin are between the riparian states, the SADC ministers who are not party to the Zambezi basin also exact some pressure on the riparians since it is SADC ministers' standing agenda. At that level, they don't just talk about co-operation in water issues but about issues including their co-operation in liberation struggles. That is the power of the regional approach.

At a functional level, the Protocol provides the basis for joint studies, cross-sectoral co-operation, data-sharing and collecting, and to set the parameters for development activities on shared river basins. The Protocol 'is the common thread' across all of the region's river basin organisations and, biennially, SADC facilitates an RBO co-ordinating meeting so that actors across the basins can compare practices, issues and processes.

Regional policies, plans and organisations

The shift in regional thinking about water is not only reflected in international law at the regional level; it is also reflected in water's changing place in SADC(C) structures: from its being part of the Environment and Land Management Sector (ELMS), to its own Water Sector, to the present Water Division within the overarching Directorate of Infrastructure and Services. Thus water for the environment now includes water management for, among other things, economic development. Moreover, water management is embedded within wider SADC processes of regional economic development, as highlighted in the 2005 documents of the SADC Regional Indicative Strategic Development Programme and the 2011 SADC Regional Strategy for Water Resources Development and Management.

Subsidiary to the Protocol are the SADC Regional Water Policy, the Regional Water Strategy and Regional Strategic Action Plan on Integrated Water Resources Management (RSAP Phases I, II and III). The Policy highlights the various opportunities water management presents to achieving the SADC goal and objectives and the attainment of

Millennium Development Goals (MDGs). The RSAP, recently concluding its third phase, 2011–2015, guides implementation.

As highlighted in Table 5.1, SADC states are party to numerous river basin agreements and organisations (RBOs). Some agreements stretch back as far as the 1891 treaty between the colonial governments of Great Britain and Portugal on the use of Zambezi River waters. Others are the results of intra-colonial policy (e.g., between Northern and Southern Rhodesia), or between colonial states and South Africa's apartheid

---

Box 5.2   Guiding Policy and Legal Provisions in the SADC Water Sector

Regional level:
- The SADC Declaration and Treaty (1992)
- The SADC Regional Indicative Strategic Development Plan (2005)
- The SADC Revised Protocol on Shared Watercourses (2000)
- The SADC Regional Water Policy (2006)
- The SADC Regional Water Strategy (2007)
- The Southern African Vision for Water, Life and the Environment in the Twenty-first Century (2006)
- The SADC Regional Awareness and Communication Strategy for the Water Sector (2010)
- Climate Change Adaptation in SADC: A Strategy for the Water Sector (2011)
- The SADC Regional Strategic Action Plans (1999, 2004 and 2010); and
- The SADC Guidelines for Strengthening River Basin Organisations (2010)

At the international level:
- The Copenhagen Declaration (1991)
- The Dublin Principles (1992)
- Agenda 21 of the UN Conference on Environment and Development (1992)
- The UN Convention on the Law of Non-Navigational Uses of International Watercourses (1997); and
- The Millennium Development Goals (MDGs) (2000)

Source: SADC (2012).

government (e.g., between Portugal and the Republic of South Africa on the development of the Cunene river basin in 1969). The RSAP III states that joint management institutions have been arrived at in all shared basins in the region, though it appears to me that this is something of an exaggeration (see Table 5.1). Far from being isolated entities, these RBOs have become 'incubators' of global water governance, involving a range of actors from stream-level smallholder farmers to European and North American resource management 'experts' and representatives of riparian states. Indeed, a serious and valid criticism of SADC in general, and the water division in particular, is the organisation's absolute financial, technical and human capital dependence on developed country partners, international financial institutions, intergovernmental organisations and (local and global) consultants and think tanks for both programming and project implementation. I encourage the reader to visit the SADC Water Sector ICP (International Collaborating Partner) Collaboration Portal at http://www.icp-confluence-sadc.org/icp-projects for details of the ways and means entities such as the African Development Bank, AusAID, DfID, DANIDA, SIDA, NORAD and BMZ are actively engaged in water resources management and development in the region.

The agreements shown in Table 5.1 are mainly those that form basin-wide arrangements – ORASECOM and ZAMCOM, for instance. However, numerous other bilateral and multilateral agreements exist, mainly between South Africa and its co-riparians in various basins the country shares with other states. While many of the historical agreements are not 'satisfactory' by today's needs and standards, they nevertheless form the basis for discussion on how to move forward for mutual benefit sharing. Joint management authorities, for example the Lesotho Highlands Development Commission (LHDC) between South Africa and Lesotho, the Joint Permanent Technical Committee (JPTC) between South Africa, Mozambique and Swaziland, and the Zambezi River Authority (ZRA) between Zambia and Zimbabwe, concern specific projects involving development and management of hydraulic infrastructure. These joint management authorities are not basin-wide. Initiatives such as the Lesotho Highlands Water Project (LHWP) are regularly put forward by scholars as positive examples of the potential for regional co-operation on water resources to result in multipurpose and mutually beneficial outcomes. This is despite the undeniable environmental and social costs of the exercise. Most recently, as reported in the national daily newspaper *Mmegi*, Botswana's ability to draw 495 MCM/yr from the Chobe/Zambezi system has been lauded by Kitso Mokaila, the country's former Minister of Minerals, Energy and Water Resources, as the result of its participation in ZAMCOM.

Pluses and minuses

The SADC's self-stated aim is 'the attainment of an integrated regional economy on the basis of balance, equity and mutual benefit for all Member States. The SADC goal is premised on the three key objectives of poverty eradication, food security and economic development' (see http://www.sadc.int/about-sadc/overview/). The centrality of IWRM-based transboundary water resources management to the attainment of these goals is obvious. The SADC highlights the comparative deficiencies of the region relative to the rest of the world, as shown in Table 5.2.

As shown in Table 5.2, from a SADC policy-maker's point of view, the enduring underdevelopment of the region is partly a function of uncaptured water resources. In comparison with their developed state counterparts, the SADC as a whole on a per capita basis withdraws only one-eighth of available renewable water supplies. In percentage terms, when compared with developed states, SADC captures no more than one-fifth of this water and irrigates a mere one-tenth of the region's irrigable land. In terms of potable water supply and improved sanitation, SADC state performance falls far below world averages, let alone developed state averages.

From a SADC policy-maker's perspective, then, much of the region's problems can be solved through improved infrastructure: pipes, dams, canals and so on. Hence the logic of placing the Water Division within the Infrastructure Division. From a politician's perspective, the supply-side value is also clear: 'this pipeline is brought to you by your government'. And from a private company's perspective, SADC states' expressed desire

Table 5.2   Comparison of SADC water sector status with other world benchmarks/ indicators

Sector	SADC Status	World Averages	Developed World Status
Water abstraction	170 m³/cap/yr	570 m³/cap/yr	1 330 m³/cap/yr
Surface water storage	14 per cent of available renewable water resources (ARWR)	25 per cent of ARWR stored	70–90 per cent of ARWR stored
Irrigated land	7 per cent irrigated of available irrigable land	20 per cent irrigated of available irrigable land	70 per cent irrigated of available irrigable land
Water supply	61 per cent of SADC population has access to an adequate and safe water supply	87 per cent of the world population (2006) has access to an adequate and safe water supply	100 per cent of the population has access to an adequate and safe water supply
Sanitation	39 per cent of SADC population has access to an adequate sanitation service	62 per cent of the world population (2006) has access to an adequate sanitation service	100 per cent of the population has access to an adequate sanitation service

Source: SADC (2012: 6).

to capture their resources appears to be highly profitable. So, not only across the SADC region, but across all of sub-Saharan Africa, addressing persistent water problems looks very much like a renewed hydraulic mission; big infrastructure for big (shareable) benefits. The SADC Water Sector Implementation Plan is slated to proceed in three phases. Phase 1 (2013–2017) focuses on institutional reform, capacity-building, project preparation and implementation. The associated cost is estimated to be US$16 billion. Phase 2 (2018–2022) will focus on implementation, capacity-building and monitoring and evaluation at a cost of US$104 billion. SADC estimates that the Implementation Plan will be 40 per cent complete by the end of Phase 2. Phase 3 (2023–2027) will also focus on implementation, capacity-building, monitoring and evaluation and has an associated cost of US$80 billion. SADC states that the plan will be 100 per cent completed at the end of Phase 3. An overview of SADC's Vision 2027 for the water sector is shown in Table 5.3.

In order to achieve these goals, the SADC has prioritised a number of projects it defines as regional (RG), transboundary or 'cross-border' (XB), and national priority (P). These are itemised in Table 5.4.

In addition to the 23 functionally oriented projects articulated at Maseru, an additional 11 – defined as 'gap projects' – have been prioritised to address specific challenges across the Water Division's three priority areas or, as the SADC calls them, the three pillars: water governance and institutional reform, infrastructure development, and water management. All of these gap projects reflect problems with institutional reform. Finance for these projects was discussed at the

Table 5.3 Water sector vision 2027 targets

Sector	Current Status	Vision 2027 Targets
Surface water storage	14 per cent of ARWR stored	25 per cent of ARWR stored to meet SADC regional demand; eventual target is 75 per cent stored, as world benchmark is 70–90 per cent of ARWR stored
Agriculture	3.4 million hectares irrigated (7 per cent of potential)	10 million hectares irrigated (20 per cent of potential); world average is 20 per cent
Hydropower	12 GW installed (8 per cent of potential)	75 GW installed (50 per cent of potential) to meet SAPP targets and exports to other RECs
Water supply	61 per cent of 260 million people served	75 per cent of 350 million people served; eventual target is 100 per cent served
Sanitation	39 per cent of 260 million people served	75 per cent of 350 million people served; eventual target is 100 per cent served
Water abstraction	44 km³/yr abstracted	264 km³/yr abstracted to meet expected increase in water demand

Source: SADC (2012: 2)8.

Table 5.4   Water sector priority projects as identified at the Maseru conference 2011

1	Regional Projects	
RG-1	Inga III Hydropower	DRC, electric power shared regionally
RG-2	Lesotho Highlands Phase II	Lesotho, South Africa
RG-3	Batoka George Hydropower Scheme	Zambia, Zimbabwe
RG-4	Songwe River Basin Development Project	Malawi, Tanzania
2	**Cross-Border Projects**	
XB-1	Upper Okavango Food Security	Angola, Namibia
XB-2	Vaal-Gamagara Water Supply	Botswana, South Africa
XB-3	Ressano Garcia Weir	Mozambique, South Africa
XB-4	Lomahasho-Namaacha Water Supply	Swaziland, Mozambique
XB-5	Water Supply and Sanitation to 12 Locations	Angola, Botswana, DRC, Malawi, Mozambique, Tanzania, Zambia, Zimbabwe
3	**National Priority Projects**	
P-1	Water Supply and Sanitation – Lubango Phase 2	Angola
P-2	Limpopo Basin Water Monitoring	Botswana
P-3	Water Supply and Sanitation – Kinshasa	DRC
P-4	Lesotho Lowlands Water Supply Scheme – Zone 1	Lesotho
P-5	Mombezi Multi-purpose Dam	Malawi
P-6	Water Supply – 13 Housing Estates	Mauritius
P-7	Movene Dam	Mozambique
P-8	Artificial Recharge of Windhoek Aquifer – Phases 2B and 3	Namibia
P-9	Reducing Non-Revenue Water and Increasing Use Efficiency	Seychelles
P-10	Demand Management in 62 Urban Centres	South Africa
P-11	Nodvo Dam	Swaziland
P-12	Ruhuhu Valley Irrigation Scheme	Tanzania
P-13	Climate Change Adaptation to Drought – Agro-ecological Region 1	Zambia
P-14	Bulawayo-Zambezi Water Supply Scheme	Zimbabwe

Source: SADC (2012: 34).

SADC Infrastructure Investment Conference in Maputo in June 2013, and further explored at the SADC Summit of Heads of State and Government, held in Lilongwe in August 2013. In addition to seed finance largely derived from donors and private sector lenders, what has also emerged out of this extended planning process is a serious critique from the left and from grassroots, in particular the Southern African People's Solidarity Network, which organises a 'SADC People's Summit' parallel to the annual SADC Summit. Their argument is that what SADC regards as a 'plus' – i.e., being 'open for business' with the private sector and donor states in line with neoliberal globalisation – is a 'minus' for the region's people.

Whenever asked to explain the persistent difficulty with implementation, both at national and regional levels, Lewis Jonker, formerly of the University of the Western Cape, was fond of saying, 'If you are always planning, then you are never failing.' In his view, what is holding back progress in effective 'institutional orientation and configuration' is the fear of failure among the region's and each individual nation's politicians. The cost of 'getting it wrong' will be a stain on the personal record and possibly a loss of political power at the polls. In my view, this is no doubt true, but it fails to tell the whole story, which requires us to reflect back on what was discussed in Chapter 2 – that the nature of the African state is such that those in power stand to lose too much from a meaningful and fundamental shift away from the status quo. The 'pluses' in SADC planning and implementation processes toward shared watercourses reflect areas that either do not challenge but rather reinforce state-centric authority; and/or do not threaten those who hold political, economic and social power within national and regional configurations of social forces. Remember that the global governance agenda for water argues for fundamental shifts: away from the state to the river basin as territorial space for decision-making; away from elites to stakeholders as the authors of decisions; and away from technical experts serving the state, to inclusive forms of knowledge including citizen science and indigenous perspectives. We are a long way from this in the southern African region.

Let's turn to a few examples. In the 2012 Regional Infrastructure Development Master Plan, the SADC argues that the region needs more bilateral or trilateral water infrastructure-specific agreements that deliver real-time benefits, such as the Zambezi River Authority (ZRA), the Komati Basin Water Authority (KOBWA) and the Lesotho Highlands Water Commission consisting of the Lesotho Highlands Development Authority (LHDA) in Lesotho and the Trans-Caledon Tunnel Authority in South Africa (TCTA). The academic world seems to agree, citing these as clear examples of transboundary 'benefit sharing' and regional 'peace building'. Each authority focuses on the operation and maintenance of large-scale infrastructure: the Kariba Dam in the middle Zambezi; the Katse and Mohale dams in the highlands of Lesotho; and the Maguga and Driekoppies dams in Swaziland and South Africa respectively. Each of these dams is multipurpose, providing a mix of two or more of hydropower generation, flow regulation, water supply for irrigated agriculture, cities and industry, and tourism and recreation. These activities clearly reinforce state power and deliver benefits to dominant actors in each state. In this era of new large-scale water infrastructure building, it is easy to forget the 'minuses' felt by local people who lost land and livelihoods to each of these impoundment projects and the protests they staged in support of a losing cause. The displacement of the Batonga from their ancestral lands during the construction of the Kariba Dam is perhaps the most well-known case for the worst way to build a dam, but was all too typical in the 1950s. Some 20 000 people were resettled in the case of the Lesotho Highlands, but International Rivers reports that another 150 000 people were negatively affected downstream. The Maguga Dam, built in the early part of the twenty-first century, followed a process quite different from both the Katse and Kariba projects. Significantly fewer households were impacted and those that were were centrally involved in the planning of their resettlement and compensation packages. This suggests that local people at the periphery of state power and authority do not necessarily have to lose out absolutely in every case. At the same time, however, there can be no doubt that the main beneficiaries of these dams are not those who occupied the lands inundated through the projects.

All sorts of wild schemes for damming and diverting the waters of the region are on the cards for SADC policy-makers. For example, it was long the vision of Namibia's former President Sam Nujoma to divert the waters of the Congo River to Namibia. Initially, in the late 1990s, his idea was to divert water from the mouth of the river and bring it by pipeline and canal all the way to Namibia. When it became clear that this was sheer folly, the idea shifted to the headwaters where it would be much easier to channel water from this point into the Cuito/Cubango system and eventually 'green the desert' lands of the Kalahari. When Nujoma's office presented the project idea to Namibia's Ministry of Agriculture, Water and Rural Development, it was sent back as socially and ecologically unfeasible. The response from Nujoma's office was: we do not care about this; just estimate what it will cost. There are numerous plans for inter-basin transfer schemes across the region – the Namibian National Eastern Water Carrier project in Namibia; the North-South Carrier Project in Botswana; the National Matabeleland Zambezi Water Transfer project in Zimbabwe, which may also supply Botswana and South Africa – many of them 'policed' by donor states and influential environmental NGOs such as Conservation International and International Rivers. However, this policing notwithstanding, where the interests of private sector actors (big agriculture and big industry, especially mining), the state (central government in particular) and powerful interest groups (big cities) coalesce around the perceived need for water, the evidence across the region shows that the project – irrespective of global governance frameworks – will move forward. The recently agreed-to three-nation agreement to pipe water from the highlands of Lesotho, through South Africa, all the way to Botswana's capital city of Gaborone, is a case in point.

On the other side of the decision-taking coin is the unwillingness to equip and empower the river basin organisations as per their intended design. In 2010, the SADC produced, with the help of GTZ, UKaid and USAID, a series of booklets that together constitute officially sanctioned 'guidelines for strengthening river basin organisations'. Two years later, the SADC identified important 'gap projects', which primarily deal with failures and shortcomings of governance and management, pertaining not to the structure but the performance of the new water architecture. River basin organisations at both national and transboundary levels are designed to become supra-national authorities, generating their own revenues, master plans, and making allocative decisions independent of state authorities. State authorities are envisioned to play a regulatory role, setting out the governance and management framework for these organisations. Given Africa's inheritance of nonsensical colonial boundaries, transboundary basin organisations are seen by many as a logical step toward regional integration.

However, it is clear that RBOs do not come anywhere near to replacing the state as the legitimate decision-making authority where water access, use and management is concerned. Indeed, power has not been devolved to the RBO itself, but resides with each riparian state through its Commissioner. At best, then, RBOs are 'talking shops', not decision-making bodies. The Commissioners are served by a Secretariat whose primary role is to guide them in establishing an action plan for IWRM. The tendency, so far, is to utilise the Secretariat as a clearing house for projects that gather data, and generate and disseminate knowledge. Since the Secretariats across the board are understaffed and poorly financed, they then become a focal point for the countless number of consultants who pass through their doors and do the actual research (in line with government-determined terms of reference). While the head of the Secretariat can influence the shape of the action programme, it remains up to the sovereign states to decide on what they would like to do.

State actors bypass regional organisations in the name of 'sovereignty' if it is in their perceived interest to do so. For example, Malawi is the only riparian state to not ratify the Zambezi Watercourse Commission agreement. The research by Joanna Fatch of the University of Western Cape and myself in 2014 shows that Malawi treats its share of the Zambezi basin as four separate entities, with each piece of the overall basin subject to specific bilateral behaviours, actions and/or agreements: the Songwe River Basin Development Plan with Tanzania, to be made operational through the Joint Permanent Commission for Co-operation, forms the basis for significant co-operation; but the Lake Malawi border (established through colonial-era treaty) along Tanzania's shore continues to be a matter of contention, though use of the shared waters continues amicably by stakeholders there; Malawi and Mozambique have co-operative agreements on particular aspects of resource access, use and management on both Lake Malawi and the Shire-Zambezi rivers. Malawi and Mozambique established a Joint Watercourse Commission in 2003 to help shape their interactions. The government of Malawi regards the Zambezi watercourse commission not as a desirable supra-national entity, but as a possible threat to Malawi sovereignty. This is but one of many similar cases across sub-Saharan Africa, from Lake Chad to Lake Victoria, and from the Limpopo River to the Volta River. In our view, such sub-basin behaviours are not indicators of 'fragmented policy approaches' – so constituting a 'failure' when analysed from a neo-institutionalist perspective – but of a coherent and relatively successful approach aimed at satisfying 'the national interest' as determined by government officials.

To be sure, the SADC Protocol on Shared Watercourses is a unique document on the African continent. Shaped in terms of the UN Convention on Non-Navigational Uses of International Watercourses, it is legally binding and commits SADC member states to the pursuit of 'equitable and reasonable use' of the region's shared watercourses. As shown here, it is highly regarded by regional policy-makers, scholars and water professionals. In line with the predominance of sovereignty, however, member states reserve the right to act in their 'national interest', agreements made prior to the enforcement of the Protocol are exempt from the Protocol, and members may opt out of the agreement if they so wish (though peer pressure is likely, in my view, to keep them in line). Member states regularly invoke the Protocol when entering into bilateral or trilateral arrangements, while bypassing the relevant watercourse commission of which they are members. Granted, the commission shapes water and related resource-use decisions within the context of the basin, but the basin organisation rarely if ever determines the feasibility of these activities. Indeed, in the context of the Orange-Senqu river basin commission, South Africa sidesteps 'the basin' by dealing with Lesotho separately (upper Orange) from its relations with Namibia (lower Orange). Botswana, as a non-water contributing member, participates in joint studies and so on, but the day-to-day hard bargaining excluded them up until a multi-state, mutually beneficial water transfer scheme shifted to the foreground. Clearly, all SADC states tend to behave the same way: where national interests are likely to be affected, they will approach the relevant riparian state actor at that time. According to one senior RBO official, in governments' eyes the Secretariat is the scapegoat when things go wrong, while the Commissioners regard themselves as the 'heroes' when things go right.

Moderating and shaping behaviour

Granted, many of the bilateral and trilateral projects are important and have multiple beneficiaries across the conventional divides of race, class and gender, particularly in cities, but less so in rural areas where dual economies continue to predominate. Given the ill fit of human settlement patterns (highlands and coasts) with water endowments, there is no doubt that the needs of the region's cities will become the dominant driver of water infrastructure development over time. As shown in the SADC plans here, big infrastructure – from dams to roads and ports – is the new regional honeypot. But, as suggested here, global governance discourses continue to shape the way development plans are packaged. They are particularly influential since much of the SADC's regional integration agenda is bankrolled by foreigners. In their important study of advocacy networks in international politics, Margaret Keck and Kathryn Sikkink (1999) describe these as 'norm entrepreneurs', who act in many ways as knowledge brokers in the region. Indeed, the region's water reforms – from laws and policies to institutional configurations – closely mirror global thinking as it has developed from Stockholm to Copenhagen to Dublin, Rio, Bonn and beyond: so while IWRM and the Dublin Principles provide the overarching conceptual framework, much of the actual work on the ground – i.e., data gathering, knowledge disseminating, human resource capacity-building – is shaped through donor state interests, which change often dramatically over time.

In the first decade after the end of the Cold War, the agenda concerned implementing IWRM through new river basin organisations, an exercise that is ongoing as those at the centre of the region's constellation of power – and much to the chagrin of regional bureaucrats and water professionals who firmly believe in the logic and value of IWRM – play a delicate game of (largely feigned) acquiescence and (mostly stalwart) resistance. Subsequent projects and programmes have focused on, to name but several of many: stakeholder participation, water demand management, gender mainstreaming, anti-corruption, indigenous knowledge, water accounting, groundwater governance, ecosystem services, the economics of water, disaster management and risk reduction, water security and the green economy and, most recently, climate change adaptation.

This is not to suggest that these exercises are futile or unwarranted. To the contrary, the logic of their dissemination is impeccable. Some of these exercises have reaped valuable and demonstrable benefits: baseline information, knowledge dissemination, human resource capacity development, the extension of these norms to a new generation of citizens, scholars and policy-makers across the region, and numerous (relatively inclusive) platforms for discussion. My advice to donors is to keep giving and to keep pushing, but to also listen more carefully to the many voices in the region.

Conclusion
Across the SADC, when and where agreements are struck regarding the sharing of transboundary waters, they serve to reinforce the existing social configurations of power within states, within the region, and around the world. Overwhelmingly they are about power: enhancing the power of the state through large-scale, hydraulic-mission-style infrastructure development. Rare is the 'deal' that strengthens the weak or places the marginalised at the centre of benefits. If the poor benefit, they do so either as an accidental by-product of inter-state actions or

because they pushed themselves onto the agenda (often with the help of international NGOs), or because state actors were pressured by more powerful international actors such as the European Union (EU) or Nordic donors to ensure pro-poor or gender-sensitive design. The poor state, too, finds the rewards of regional water co-operation to be as thin as gruel: Lesotho upstream and Namibia downstream of South Africa on the Orange-Senqu, and Mozambique downstream of everyone.

Southern Africa serves as a mostly willing subject for global experiments in IWRM and good water governance. The SADC's long-standing relationship with the EU and the Nordics, which began in the late 1970s in the struggle against apartheid, ensures an endless stream of money, technology, expertise and comradely goodwill. The nature of the region's political economy demands fundamental reforms in the way water is used and by whom. But, paradoxically, it is also this political economy which, in the context of neoliberal globalisation, encourages decision-makers to stay the course: more mines, more cash crops, and less deliberate state intervention on behalf of those most in need. So the 'institutional configurations and orientations' remain centred on the sovereign state, with state governors being the recognised seat of decision-taking authority, and with (often foreign) expert knowledge constituting the scientific and technical basis for action. We remain, unfortunately, a long way from the IWRM/good governance ideal.

Conclusion

A Glass Half Full
In Pursuit of Clinical Politics

When I first drafted this conclusion, there was a hailstorm in Auckland Park, Johannesburg. The rains were a bit late, but it all felt pretty normal. It also felt pretty normal when the power went out, there was flash flooding, and in the poorest locations, due to poor sanitation, there was a spike in the number of cases of dysentery. Why is this normal? Or, rather, why do I perceive this to be normal? And I am not alone. The grumbling across the greater metropolitan area was and remains palpable; it can be heard like the rumble of thunder off in the distance: the government is to blame. When I moved from Gaborone to Maun in 2004, the advice from the expatriate community was to not depend on the state: sink your own borehole, look after your own septic system, burn or bury your organic waste, hire in a private contractor to sort out the rest. Across sub-Saharan Africa it is much the same: as you move from chaotic central business districts to the leafy suburbs – of Harare, Maputo, Luanda, Nairobi, Kampala, Addis Ababa, and all the way across to Lagos and Dakar – the noise of diesel generators is almost deafening. Public water quality not up to scratch? Buy bottled. And let's not even talk about waterborne sewerage and sanitation. This is water in its social context. As I said at the outset of this book, water resource access, use and management are nothing less than a mirror of the society back to itself. That people either choose or are compelled to look after themselves, as individuals or communities, and bypass, avoid or ignore the state says a great deal not only about governance but about the social relations of production: who has power, on what basis and why. That being said, one should not be surprised by the two faces of southern

Africa, Sandton and Alexandra, Constantia and Khayelitsha, profitable agribusiness and less than 1 t/ha smallholder farmer.

As I revisit and rewrite sections of this conclusion – at the same table in Auckland Park albeit 16 months later – the region is at the tail-end of a severe El Niño-driven drought. Millions of SADC citizens are food insecure and in desperate need of drought relief. The international donor community is being mobilised for action. Yet drought is normal, as is flood. As the saying goes, there is no 'average rainfall' in the region; look at a time-series hydrograph and you will see that it is always a case of feast or famine. If there is water scarcity, it is socially constructed, not naturally limited. Proper planning and storage means continued profits for big agriculture, even during the worst of the drought. Water is renewable; there is plenty of it, more than enough for everyone. Yet when there is a shortage we focus on the shacks and the 1 t/ha farmers as if their lack of access to basic services and resources of all types is somehow indicative of Africa's natural condition. We see the images and say, 'See, water is scarce and we are running out.' We forget about the big farmers, who always seem to have enough.

Today we complicate this discourse with fear of the impacts of climate change. Perhaps unintentionally, then, these narratives drive policy along a resource capture pathway: if you have it, you better keep it; if you don't, you better get it. Because states dominate the governance space, the 'keeping' and the 'getting' are framed through the 'national interest of sovereign states' lenses. As such, governments of the day either do nothing (afraid to fail; afraid to succeed) or choose the easy path – the high-tech supply-side option – or, where they can't be bothered or simply aren't interested, let the NGOs and community groups do it themselves.

In this book I have articulated different ways of seeing the resource and new ways of managing it. These different ways of seeing the resource – green, blue, virtual – help reframe the question of how much water there is, thereby widening the policy options space. At the same time, the late-modern discourse of IWRM makes a strong case for locating the decision space within the river basin, extending authority from the state to all relevant stakeholders, and for basing decisions on inclusive forms of knowledge: everybody's experience counts.

I have encouraged the reader to ponder five key points: (1) our water problems are human made so fatalism should have no place in resource management; (2) urban water is small water, so lack of access is a political issue not a natural scarcity issue; (3) green water shows us that food security can result from better crop choices; (4) far from water wars, what we see is inter-state co-operation, which is to be celebrated and encouraged, but we should also know that co-operation often reflects deals among unequals; and (5) the real water war is ongoing, and it is against the poor.

Taken together, in my view, such insights and reframings provide the SADC region with an opportunity to pursue a hydraulic mission with equity, efficiency and sustainability firmly at the centre of decision-making. There are many opportunities to do things better, for people, for nature, and for states.

The region, as I have shown, is hobbled by its history – of its inclusion into global capitalism through resource extraction and social exclusion, of wasted decades spent fighting while other parts of the world, such as Korea, were turning the global Great Boom into the foundation for economic and social development, and by the contemporary neoliberal setting that is wedded to a facilitative rather than determinative state approach to economic and social development. This is all fine for those at the top of the food chain; but, as the data shows, it is not good at all for everyone else. However, would the current world order be willing, one doubts the leadership capabilities across the region: conservative and patriarchal at best, kleptocratic and xenophobic at worst. But let's not place all of the blame on SADC state governors; if the region is badly governed, as I argue it is, it is badly *globally governed*. The African 'big man' at home is treated as, and generally willingly behaves as, the 'small boy' abroad. In 1990, James Ferguson wrote *The Anti-Politics Machine* about development aid in Lesotho. In that book, he showed how failure of development projects is expected and pre-explained by the donors. So, where donors believe you are incapable of succeeding with the plan as developed by them, recipients are free to do what they want, which, in the Lesotho case meant using aid money to reinforce extant social relations of power, not reconfigure them. And would you do any different? I know I wouldn't.

Force fed a constantly changing diet of development projects and programmes – pro-poor development today, climate change adaptation tomorrow – while suited up in the straightjacket of cross-conditionalities, is it any wonder that SADC state leaders have cantered over to China for money and technical expertise that arrives with no strings attached?

The SADC states have gained a great deal of attention and positive reinforcement for their willingness to co-operate in transboundary waters. Many a European Master's and PhD thesis has been written about benefit sharing in this or that basin, about this or that RBO as evidence of a functionalist, neo-institutional regime, and so on. At the same time, an equal number of studies have lamented the incapacity of states to deliver 'small water' to their large urban and peri-urban populations. Rare is the attempt to juxtapose the two and ask: of what is this an example? More often than not, the former is explained as an instance of good governance and best practice (enter the private sector to build the dams), while the latter is explained as a lack of capacity, so needing aid and assistance (enter the private sector to install the management and delivery devices). In my view, these examples are two sides of the same coin. Taken together, the total performance (inter-state co-operation, intra-state delivery failure) reflects the configuration of social forces within and among states within southern Africa and the world.

In response to this explanation, an average political scientist would say that this is power politics, pure and simple. So the rich have water in abundance, while the poor make do with whatever they can. Is this not the way things have always been? Such a cynical perspective usually emanates from someone who has a secure water supply and a functioning flush toilet. But that's the point: the wealthy are not arguing about water *per se*; they are arguing about what water will do for them

– generate income through industry, mining and manufacturing, and irrigated agriculture. This is what we see across SADC states. The poor, on the other hand, are arguing about water for their own immediate consumption. As an activist academic, I refuse to play the cynic. Since most citizens across the SADC region are either poor, or poorly served by their state, it is in the interests of SADC state leaders to change this condition. Ultimately everyone is downstream, meaning that if you abuse those downstream long enough they will become your problem. The new-millennial rise of social movements across the world is testimony to this. So, what to do? In my view, rather than adhere to a cynical viewpoint (get mine, forget about the rest), it is imperative that those interested in IWRM practise what Robert Cox (1996) described as clinical politics. Make inroads where possible, aim for the lowest hanging fruit. How to know what to do? What I have taken to asking my students to do, in their essays and presentations, is to show me where things work – anywhere in the world – and to ask questions. Why does it work? Is it fungible, meaning would it work to the benefit of all in southern Africa? And, if you believe it will, then give it a try and do not be afraid to fail.

In bringing this book to a close, and in rounding off this argument, I want to offer five explanations as to why some things have worked to the general benefit of citizens. Many positive things have happened in water resources management and governance in the SADC region since the nearly co-terminus ends of the Cold War and apartheid nearly 25 years ago. I will group them under five general categories.

Water is regarded as a technical field

Because water is in everything, it tends to be disregarded as a litmus test for regional governance and state stability. Rather, state leaders understand the role of water in the economy and recognise it as an 'expert science' requiring highly skilled personnel. It was on the back of this perception that WaterNet was created in the late 1990s as a joint SADC-EU initiative under the guidance of the Netherlands, who at the time held the presidency of the EU. WaterNet is a regional research and training programme that brings young people and established water professionals together from around the region and the world to conduct and publish joint research, exchange information and participate in a regional Master's degree in IWRM. A great deal of knowledge has been generated and disseminated through increasingly user-friendly platforms. Several hundred students have now been trained in this, and related, programmes. In my view, this constitutes the future leadership base for water resources governance and management in the region. They are armed with a new way of thinking. This is social change that flies under the political radar.

There Is No Alternative (TINA)

The example I have given of the City of Cape Town's positive engagement with shack dwellers suggests to me that this is a municipality with no alternative. Supported by the Constitution and government policy, it is not possible to simply sweep these people aside. Instead, an important contact point has been established between the state (through the municipality) and civil society, through community organisations and wider national NGOs, which helps address the serious trust deficit that exists between the South African state and civil society. Granted, it is a small victory, but it is 'win-win', not zero sum. We must look for other opportunities to enhance the relations between the state and civil society, and this is most likely to happen at the level of the municipality or district where government meets the people through service delivery.

Mutual vulnerability

Evidence shows that the further a decision-maker is from the negative consequences of his or her decision, the less likely he or she is to change the behaviour. So, central state decisions on the building of large dams such as the Narmada in India negatively affect millions where the land will be inundated, but they have no such negative impact on those who made the decision or on the new beneficiaries of the development project. Where decision-makers are also vulnerable, positive outcomes are possible: so the North-South Carrier 1 and 2, which brings water to Gaborone, where the powerful live, will benefit others directly by virtue of their presence in the capital city or because they constitute part of the politician's constituency along the route of the pipeline.

The politician looks good

Politicians understand two things: money and votes. Even neo-authoritarian states with false, faulty or failing democratic processes know that decisions that enhance their power are always welcome. In Botswana, it was a wise move by the Kalahari Conservation Society to make Ian Khama their patron many years ago. Now as president, the conservation movement has a powerful ally in its corner.

You are not alone

Globalisation has many different faces, both negative and positive. One of the positive faces is the ability of marginalised groups to network through increasingly ubiquitous and affordable ICT. There are also many direct face-to-face opportunities for people to organise and exchange views, at very different levels in society: from slum dwellers' associations to bureaucrat training exercises to student and staff exchanges across South-South and North-South landscapes.

The water world is caught between the 'is' and the 'ought': through neoliberal globalisation we continue to dam, divert and drain the resource while codifying these actions through the physical and legal space of the sovereign state. Governments, supported by technical experts, continue to drive development frameworks, projects and practices. Across sub-Saharan Africa this is often characterised as 'Africa Rising', but to me it looks a lot like neocolonial extractivism. At the same time, we have arrived at the globally sanctioned discourse of IWRM: that for equitable, sustainable and efficient water resource use we must scale our actions to the river basin, let stakeholders take the decisions, and base these decisions on inclusive forms of knowledge. Antonio Gramsci (1971) described this as 'the interregnum' where the old is dying, but the new is not yet born. To me this is a time of great uncertainty but also of great possibility. Let us not be accepting of flash floods, dysentery, power failures; let us not be cynical, but rather clinical in the pursuit of some water for all forever.

Select Bibliography

African Ministerial Committee on Water (AMCOW). 2012. *Water Security and Climate Resilient Development: Strategic Framework*. Abuja, Nigeria: AMCOW and Stockholm Global Water Partnership.

Allan, J.A. 1998. 'Virtual Water: A Strategic Resource: Global Solutions to Regional Deficits'. *Groundwater* 36(4): 545–6.

———. 2002. 'Hydro-peace in the Middle East: Why No Water Wars? A Case Study of the Jordan River Basin'. *SAIS Review* 22(2): 255–72.

———. 2003. 'IWRM/IWRAM: A New Sanctioned Discourse?' Occasional paper 50, April. SOAS Water Issues Study Group, London.

———. 2011. *Virtual Water*. London: I.B. Tauris.

Ashton, P.J. 2000. 'Southern African Water Conflicts: Are They Inevitable or Preventable?' In *Water Wars: Enduring Myth or Impending Reality?* African Dialogue Monograph Series No. 2, edited by H. Solomon and A.R. Turton. Durban: ACCORD.

———. 2002. 'Avoiding Conflicts Over Africa's Water Resources'. *Ambio* 31(3): 236–42.

Assies, W. 2003. 'David Versus Goliath in Cochabamba: Water Rights, Neoliberalism, and the Revival of Social Protest in Bolivia'. *Latin American Perspectives* 130(3): 14–36.

Barraque, B. (ed.). 2011. *Urban Water Conflicts*. Abingdon, UK: CRC Press.

Bernauer, T., T Böhmelt and V. Koubi. 2012. 'Environmental Changes and Violent Conflict'. *Environmental Research Letters* 7(1).

Biswas, A.K. 2006. 'Water Management for Major Urban Centres'. *Water Resources Development* 22(2): 183–97.

———. 2008. 'Integrated Water Resources Management: Is It Working?' *Water Resources Development* 24(1): 5–22.

Bond, P. 2002. *Unsustainable South Africa*. Pietermaritzburg: University of KwaZulu-Natal Press.

———. 2008. 'The Case of Johannesburg Water: What Really Happened at the Pre-paid "Parish Pump"'. *Law, Democracy and Development* 12(1): 1–28.

———. 2013. 'Water Rights, Commons and Advocacy Narratives'. *South African Journal of Human Rights* 29(1): 126–44.

Bowman, Larry W. 1968. 'The Subordinate State System of Southern Africa'. *International Studies Quarterly* 12(3): 231–61.

Buhaug, H., N.P. Gleditsch and O.M. Theisen. 2010. 'Implications of Climate Change for Armed Conflict'. In *The Social Dimension of Climate Change: Equity and Vulnerability in a Warming World*, edited by R. Means and A. Norton. Washington, D.C.: World Bank.

Callaghy, T. 1987. 'The State as Lame Leviathan: The Patrimonial Administrative State in Africa'. In *The African State in Transition*, edited by Z. Ergas. London: Macmillan.

Chenje, M. (ed.). 2000. *State of the Environment in the Zambezi Basin 2000*. Maseru/Lusaka/Harare: SADC/IUCN/ZRA/SARDC.

Chenje, M. and P. Johnson (eds). 1994. *State of the Environment in Southern Africa*. Harare/Maseru: SARDC/SADC.

———. 1996. *Water in Southern Africa*. Harare/Maseru: SARDC/SADC.

Cheru, F. 1997. 'Global Apartheid and the Challenge to Civil Society: Africa in the Transformation of World Order'. In *The New Realism: Perspectives on Multilateralism and World Order*, edited by R. Cox. London: Macmillan.

Clapham, C. 1996. *Africa and the International System: The Politics of State Survival.* Cambridge: Cambridge University Press.

Collier, P. and Hoeffler, A. 1998. 'On the Economic Causes of Civil War'. *Oxford Economic Papers* 50(4): 563–73.

———. 2002. 'On the Incidence of Civil War in Africa'. *Journal of Conflict Resolution* 46(1): 13–28.

———. 2004. 'Greed and Grievance in Civil War'. *Oxford Economic Papers* 56: 663–95.

Conca, K. 2006. *Governing Water*. Cambridge, Mass: MIT Press.

Conley, A. 1996. 'A Synoptic View of Water Resources in Southern Africa. In *Sink or Swim? Water, Resource Security and State Co-operation*, IDP Monograph Series No. 6, edited by H. Solomon. Pretoria: Institute for Defence Policy.

Cox, R. 1987. *Production, Power and World Order: Social Forces in the Making of History*. New York: Columbia University Press.

———. 1996. *Approaches to World Order*. Cambridge: Cambridge University Press.

Cullis, J. and B. van Koppen. 2009. 'Applying the Gini Coefficient to Measure Inequality of Water Use in the Olifants River Water Management Area, South Africa'. In *Transboundary Water Governance in Southern Africa: Examining Underexplored Dimensions*, edited by L.A. Swatuk and L. Wirkus. Baden-Baden: Nomos Publishers.

Dalby, S. 2012. 'Afterword: Ecoviolence, Security, Geopolitics'. In *Environmental Change, Natural Resources and Social Conflict*, edited by M.A. Schnurr and L.A. Swatuk. Palgrave: Macmillan.

Davies, B. and J. Day. 1998. *Vanishing Waters*. Cape Town: University of Cape Town Press.

Du Pisani, A. 2001. 'New Sites of Governance: Regimes and the Future of Southern Africa'. In *Theory, Change and Southern Africa's Future*, edited by P. Vale, L.A. Swatuk and B. Oden. London: Palgrave.

Falkenmark, M. 1986. 'Fresh Water: Time for a Modified Approach'. *Ambio* 15(4): 192–200.

———. 2001. 'The Greatest Water Problem: The Inability to Link Environmental Security, Water Security and Food Security'. *International Journal of Water Resources Development* 17(4): 539–54.

Falkenmark, M. and J. Rockstrom, J. 2004. *Balancing Water for Humans and Nature: The New Approach in Ecohydrology*. London: Sterling.

Fatch, J. and L.A. Swatuk. 2014. 'Transboundary Water Politics in the Zambezi Basin: Malawi and its "Neighbors"'. Paper presented at the annual meeting of SADC/ GWP/WaterNet, Lilongwe, Malawi, 29–31 October.

Ferguson, J. 1990. *The Anti-Politics Machine: 'Development', Depoliticization and Bureaucratic Power in Lesotho*. Cambridge: Cambridge University Press.

Galtung, J. 1971. 'A Structural Theory of Imperialism'. *Journal of Peace Research* 8(2): 81–117.

Gleditsch, N.P. 2012. 'Whither the Weather? Climate Change and Conflict'. *Journal of Peace Research* 49(1): 3–9.

Gleditsch, N.P., H. Furlong, H. Hegre, B. Lacina and T. Owen. 2006. 'Conflicts Over Shared Rivers: Resource Scarcity or Fuzzy Boundaries?' *Political Geography* 25(4): 361–82.

Gleick, P. 2000a. 'Environment and Security: Water Conflict Chronology – Version 2000'. In *The World's Water 2000–2001*, edited by P. Gleick. Washington, D.C.: Island Press.

———. 2000b. *The World's Water 2000–2001: The Biennial Report on Freshwater Resources*. Washington, D.C.: Island Press.

Gramsci, A. 1971. *Selections from the Prison Notebooks*. New York: International Publishers.

Green Cross International. 2000. *Water for Peace in the Middle East and Southern Africa*. Geneva: Green Cross International.

Hanlon, J. 1986. *Beggar Your Neighbours: Apartheid Power in Southern Africa*. London: James Currey.

Herbst, J. 2000. *States and Power in Africa: Comparative Lessons in Authority and Control*. Princeton: Princeton University Press.

Heyns, P. 2003. 'Water Resources Management in Southern Africa'. In *International Waters in Southern Africa*, edited by M. Nakayama. Tokyo: United Nations University Press.

Homer-Dixon, T. 1994. 'Environmental Scarcities and Violent Conflict: Evidence from Cases'. *International Security* 19(1): 5–40.

————. 1999. *The Environment, Scarcity and Violence*. Princeton: Princeton University Press.

Iliffe, J. 1995. *Africans: The History of a Continent*. Cambridge: Cambridge University Press.

Jonker, L. 2002. 'Integrated Water Resources Management: Theory, Practice, Cases'. *Physics and Chemistry of the Earth* 27: 721–2.

————. 2005. 'IWRM: What Should We Teach? A Report on Curriculum Development at the University of the Western Cape, South Africa'. *Physics and Chemistry of the Earth* 29: 1365–73.

Jonker, L., P. van der Zaag, B. Gumbo, J. Rockstrom, D. Love and H.H.G. Savenije. 2012. 'A Regional and Multi-faceted Approach to Postgraduate Water Education: The WaterNet Experience in Southern Africa'. *Hydrology and Earth Systems Science* (HESS) 16: 4225–32.

Keck, M.E. and K. Sikkink. 1999. 'Transnational Advocacy Networks in International and Regional Politics'. *International Social Science Journal* 159: 89–101.

Keohane, R. and J. Nye. 1977. *Power and Interdependence: World Politics in Transition*. Boston: Little, Brown & Co.

Kgomotso, P. and L.A. Swatuk. 2006. 'Access to Water and Related Resources in Ngamiland, Botswana: Toward a More Critical Perspective and Sustainable Approach'. *Physics and Chemistry of the Earth* 31: 659–68.

Klaphake, A. and W. Scheumann. 2009. 'Understanding Transboundary Water Cooperation: Evidence from Sub-Saharan Africa'. In *Transboundary Water Governance in Southern Africa: Exploring Underexamined Dimensions*, edited by L.A. Swatuk and L. Wirkus. Baden-Baden: Nomos.

Konar, M., C. Dalin, S. Suweis, N. Hanasaki, A. Rinaldo and I. Rodrigues-Iturbe. 2011. 'Water for Food: The Global Virtual Water Trade Network'. *Water Resources Research* 47: 1–17.

Kujinga, K., G. Mmopelwa, C. Vanderpost and W.R.L. Masamba. 2014a. 'Short and Long Term Strategies for Household Water Insecurity in Ngamiland, Botswana'. *Journal of Sustainable Development* 7(3).

Kujinga, K., C. Vanderpost, G. Mmopelwa and P. Wolski. 2014b. 'An Analysis of Factors Contributing to Household Water Security Problems and Threats in Different Settlement Categories of Ngamiland, Botswana'. *Physics and Chemistry of the Earth* 67: 187–201.

Lautze, J. and M.A. Hanjra. 2014. 'Water Scarcity'. In *Key Concepts in Water Resource Management: A Review and Critical Evaluation*, edited by J. Lautze. London and New York: Routledge and Earthscan.

Levy, B. 2002. 'Patterns of Governance in Africa'. Africa Region Working Paper Series No. 36, September, World Bank, Washington, D.C.

Macdonald, A.M. and J. Davies. 2000. 'A Brief Review of Groundwater for Rural Water Supply in Sub-Saharan Africa'. BGS Technical Report WC/00/33. British Geological Survey, Keyworth, Nottingham, UK.

Makgetla, N. and A. Seidman. 1980. *Outposts of Monopoly Capitalism: Southern Africa in the Changing Global Economy*. London: Zed Press.

Manzungu, E. and B. Derman. 2016. 'Surges and Ebbs: National Politics and International Influence in the Formulation and Implementation of IWRM in Zimbabwe'. *Water Alternatives* 9(3): 493–512.

Mazrui, A. 1986. *The Africans: A Triple Heritage*. Boston: Little, Brown & Co.

McDonald, D. and G. Ruiters (eds). 2005. *The Age of Commodity: Water Privatization in Southern Africa*. London: Earthscan.

McKague, K., D. Wheeler, C. Cash, J. Comeault and E. Ray (eds). 2011. 'Growing Inclusive Markets'. Special Issue, *Journal of Enterprising Communities: People and Places in the Global Economy* 5(1).

Mehta, L. 2001. 'The Manufacture of Popular Perceptions of Scarcity: Dams and Water-Related Narratives in Gujarat, India'. *World Development* 29(12): 2025–41.

———. 2007. 'Whose Scarcity? Whose Property? The Case of Water in Western India'. *Land Use Policy* 24(4): 654–63.

Mehta, L., B. Derman and E. Manzungu (eds). 2016. 'Flows and Practices: The Politics of Integrated Water Resources Management (IWRM) in Southern Africa'. Special Issue, *Water Alternatives* 9(3).

Merrey, D. 2008. 'Is Normative Integrated Water Resources Management Implementable? Charting a Practical Course with Lessons from Southern Africa'. *Physics and Chemistry of the Earth* 33: 899–905.

Merrey, D., A. Prakash, L.A. Swatuk, I. Jacobs and V. Narain. 2016. 'Water Governance Futures in South Asia and Southern Africa: Déjà Vu All Over Again?' In *Freshwater Governance for the 21st Century*, edited by E. Karar. Berlin: Springer.

Mittelman, J. 1988. *Out from Underdevelopment*. London: Macmillan.

Molden, D., K. Frenken, R. Barker, C. de Fraiture, B. Mati, M. Svendsen, C. Sadoff and C.M. Finlayson. 2007. 'Trends in Water and Agricultural Development'. In *Water Food, Water for Life: A Comprehensive Assessment of Water Management in Agriculture*, edited by D. Molden. London: Earthscan.

Moore, M-L. 2013. 'Perspectives of Complexity in Water Governance: Local Experiences of Global Trends'. *Water Alternatives* 6(3): 487–505.

Mottiar, S. and P. Bond. 2012. 'The Politics of Discontent and Social Protest in Durban'. *Politikon* 39(3): 309–30.

Movik, S., L. Mehta and E. Manzungu. 2016. 'The Flow of IWRM in SADC: The Role of Regional Dynamics, Advocacy Networks and External Actors'. *Water Alternatives* 9(3): 434–55.

Mukheli, A., G. Mosupye and L.A. Swatuk. 2002. 'Is the Pungwe Water Supply Project a Solution to Water Accessibility and Sanitation Problems for the Households of Sakubva, Zimbabwe?' *Physics and Chemistry of the Earth* 27: 723–32.

Nakayama, M. (ed.). 2003. *International Waters in Southern Africa*. Tokyo: United Nations University Press.

Niang, I., O.C. Ruppel, M.A. Abdrabo, A. Essel, C. Lennard, J. Padgham and P. Urquhart. 2014. 'Africa'. In *Climate Change 2014: Impacts, Adaptation, and Vulnerability. Part B: Regional Aspects*. Contribution of Working Group II to the Fifth Assessment Report of the Intergovernmental Panel on Climate Change [edited by V.R. Barros, C.B. Field, D.J. Dokken, M.D. Mastrandrea, K.J. Mach, T.E. Bilir, M. Chatterjee, K.L. Ebi, Y.O. Estrada, R.C. Genova, B. Girma, E.S. Kissel, A.N. Levy, S. MacCracken, P.R. Mastrandrea and L.L. White]. Cambridge and New York: Cambridge University Press.

Nkiwane, S. 1988. *Destabilisation in Southern Africa: A Historical Perspective*. Dalhousie African Working Paper series. Halifax, NS: Centre for African Studies, Dalhousie University.

Noemdoe, S., L. Jonker, and L.A. Swatuk. 2007. 'Perceptions of Water Scarcity: Genadendal and Outstations'. *Physics and Chemistry of the Earth* 31: 771–8.

Nordås, R. and N.P. Gleditsch. 2007. 'Climate Change and Conflict'. *Political Geography* 26(6): 627–38.

Odumosu, T. 2000. 'When Refuse Dumps Become Mountains: Responses to Waste Management in Metropolitan Lagos'. In *The Environment and Development in Africa*, edited by M.K. Tesi. New York: Lexington.

Ohlsson, L. 1995. 'Water and Security in Southern Africa'. Publications on Water Resources No. 1. SIDA, Stockholm.

Ohlsson, L. and A.R. Turton. 1999. 'The Turning of a Screw: Social Resource Scarcity as a Bottle-neck in Adaptation to Water Scarcity'. Occasional Paper 19, April. SOAS Water Issues Study Group, London.

Ott, H., L.A. Swatuk, R. Paisley, J. Huffman, D. Ziganshina, J. Fried, D. Feldman, P. Kibel, I. Klaver, V. Maavesva and G. Ogendi. 2008. 'Common Grounds, Common Waters: Towards a Water Ethic – Roundtable Discussion Proceedings'. *Santa Clara Journal of International Law* 6: 81–111.

Palaniappan, M. and P. Gleick. 2009. 'Peak Water'. In *The World's Water, 2008–2009*, edited by P. Gleick. Washington, D.C.: Island Press.

Pressend, M. and T. Otieno (eds). 2009. *Rethinking Natural Resources in Southern Africa*. Midrand: Institute for Global Dialogue.

Rakodi, C. (ed.). 1997. *The Urban Challenge in Africa*. Tokyo: United Nations University Press.

Ramoeli, P. 2002. 'The SADC Protocol on Shared Watercourses: History and Current Status'. In *Hydropolitics in the Developing World: A Southern African Perspective*, edited by A.R. Turton and R. Henwood. Pretoria: Centre for International Political Studies.

Reisner, M. 1986. *Cadillac Desert: The American West and Its Disappearing Water.* Revised and updated. New York: Penguin.

Rijsberman, F.R. 2006. 'Water Scarcity: Fact or Fiction?' *Agricultural Water Management* 80: 5–22.

Rockstrom, J., F. Falkenmark, C. Folke, M. Lannerstad, J. Barron, E. Enfors, L. Gordon, J. Heinke, H. Hoff and C. Pahl-Wostl. 2014. *Water Resilience for Human Prosperity.* Cambridge: Cambridge University Press.

Rockstrom, J., L. Karlberg, S. Wani, J. Barron, N. Habitu, T. Oweise, A. Bruggeman, J. Farahaniand and Z. Qiang. 2010. 'Managing Water in Rainfed Agriculture: The Need for a Paradigm Shift'. *Agricultural Water Management* 97: 543–50.

Rodina, L. 2015. 'Implementation of the Human Right to Water in Khayelitsha, South Africa: Lessons from a "Lived Experience" Perspective'. IRES Working paper series No. 2015-05, University of British Columbia, Vancouver.

Rulli, M.C., A. Saviori and P. D'Odorico. 2013. 'Global Land and Water Grabbing'. *PNAS* 110(3): 892–7.

SADC, n.d. Regional Indicative Strategic Development Plan. Gaborone: SADC.

———. 2000. Protocol on Shared Watercourses in the Southern African Development Community (SADC).

———. 2005. Regional Strategic Action Plan on Integrated Water Resources Development and Management, Annotated Strategic Plan (2005–2010) (June). Gaborone: SADC.

———. 2011. Regional Strategic Action Plan on Integrated Water Resources Development and Management (2011–2015) (December). Gaborone: SADC.

———. 2012. Regional Infrastructure Development Master Plan, Water Sector Plan. Gaborone: SADC.

Sadoff, C.W. and D. Grey. 2002. 'Beyond the River: The Benefits of Cooperation on International Rivers'. *Water Policy* 4: 389–403.

Savenije, H.H.G. 2002. 'Why Water is Not an Ordinary Good, or Why the Girl is Special'. *Physics and Chemistry of the Earth* 27: 741–4.

Scanlon, J., A. Cassar and N. Nemes. 2004. 'Water as a Human Right?' IUCN Environmental Policy and Law Paper No. 51, Gland, Switzerland.

Schensul, D. and P. Heller. 2010. 'Legacies, Change and Transformation in the Post-Apartheid City: Towards an Urban Sociological Cartography'. *International Journal of Urban and Regional Research* 35(1): 78–109.

Scheumann, W. and S. Neubert (eds). 2006. *Transboundary Water Management in Africa.* Bonn: German Development Institute.

Sen, A. 1999. *Development as Freedom.* New York: Alfred A. Knopf.

Shahin, M. 2002. 'Hydrology and Water Resources in Africa'. *Water Science and Technology Library* 41. Dordrecht, Netherlands: Kluwer Academic Publishers.

Shiva, V. 2002. *Water Wars: Privatization, Pollution and Profit*. Cambridge, MA: Southend Press.

Smith, L. 2008. 'Neither Public Nor Private: Unpacking the Johannesburg Water Corporatization Model'. Social Policy and Development Programme Paper No. 27 (June). UNRISD, Geneva.

Solomon, S. 2010. *Water: The Epic Struggle for Wealth, Power and Civilization*. New York: HarperCollins.

Stockholm International Water Institute (SIWI). 2012. *The Water and Food Nexus: Trends and Development of the Research Landscape*. Stockholm: SIWI.

Swatuk, L.A. 2000. 'Power and Water: The Coming Order in Southern Africa'. In *The New Regionalism and the Future of Security and Development*, edited by B. Hettne, A. Inotai and O. Sunkel. Basingstoke: Macmillan.

———. 2002. 'Environmental Cooperation for Regional Peace and Security in Southern Africa'. In *Environmental Peacemaking*, edited by K. Conca and G.D. Dabelko. Washington, D.C.: Johns Hopkins University Press.

———. 2003. 'State Interests and Multilateral Cooperation: Thinking Strategically About Achieving "Wise Use" of the Okavango Delta System'. *Physics and Chemistry of the Earth* 28: 897–906.

———. 2008. 'A Political Economy of Water in Southern Africa'. *Water Alternatives* 1(1): 24–47.

———. 2009. 'Neoliberalism, Globalism and the Poverty Trap in Southern Africa'. In *Rethinking Natural Resources in Southern Africa*, edited by M. Pressend and T. Othieno. Midrand: Institute for Global Dialogue.

———. 2010. 'The State and Water Resources Development Through the Lens of History: A South African Case Study'. *Water Alternatives* 3(3): 521–36.

———. 2015. 'Water, Conflict and Cooperation in Southern Africa'. *WIREs Water* 2(3) (May/June): 215–30.

———. 2017. 'The Land-Water-Food-Energy Nexus: Green and Blue Water Dynamics in Contemporary Africa-Asia Relations'. In *Routledge Handbook of Africa-Asia Relations*, edited by P.A. Raposo, D. Arase and S. Cornelissen. Oxford: Routledge.

Swatuk, L.A. and J. Fatch. 2013. 'Water Resources Management and Governance in Southern Africa: Toward Regional Integration for Peace and Prosperity'. *Global Dialogue* 15(2) (Summer/Autumn), http://www.worlddialogue.org.

Swatuk, L.A and P. Kgomotso. 2007. 'The Challenges of Supplying Water to Small, Scattered Communities in the Lower Okavango Basin, Ngamiland, Botswana: An Evaluation of Government Policy and Performance'. *Physics and Chemistry of the Earth* 32: 1264–74.

Swatuk, L.A. and D. Mazvimavi. 2010. 'Water and Human Security in Africa'. In *Critical Environmental Security: Rethinking the Links Between Natural Resources and Political Violence*, edited by M. Schnurr and L.A. Swatuk. New Issues in Security No. 5. Halifax, NS: Centre for Foreign Policy Studies Monograph Series.

Swatuk, L.A., D. Mazvimavi and K. Jembere. 2010. 'Water Management for Human Security and Development in Africa'. In *Natural Resource Governance and Human Security in Africa: Emerging Issues and Trends*, edited by B. Kesselman et al. Braamfontein: Pax Africa.

Swatuk, L.A. and P. Vale. 1999. 'Why Democracy is Not Enough: Security and Development in Southern Africa in the 21st Century'. *Alternatives* 24(3): 361–89.

Swatuk, L.A. and L. Wirkus (eds). 2009. *Transboundary Water Governance in Southern Africa: Examining Underexplored Dimensions*. Baden-Baden: Nomos Publishers.

Tapela, B.N. 2012. *Social Water Scarcity and Water Use*. Pretoria: Water Research Commission.

Thompson, L. (ed.). 2014. 'Reflections on 20 Years of South African Democracy from Below'. Special Issue, *Politikon* 41(3): 335–494.

Toset, H.P.W., N.P. Gleditsch and H. Hegre. 2000. 'Shared Rivers and Interstate Conflict'. *Political Geography* 19: 971–96.

Tshabalala, T. and S. Mxobo. 2014. 'Reblocking as an Attempt at Reconfiguring and Improving Socio-economic Conditions in Informal Settlements: The Case of Mtshini Wami, Cape Town'. Planning Africa 2014: Making Great Places. Proceedings of the South African Planning Institute.

Turton, A.R. 2008. 'The Southern African Hydropolitical Complex'. In *Management of Transboundary Rivers and Lakes*, edited by A.K. Biswas, O. Varis and C. Tortajada. Berlin: Springer-Verlag.

UN-Habitat. 2013. 'State of the World's Cities 2012/13: Prosperity of Cities'. http://unhabitat.org/books/prosperity-of-cities-state-of-the-worlds-ities-20122013/.

UNDP. 1992. *Human Development Report*. New York: Oxford University Press.

———. 2010. *Human Development Report*. New York: Oxford University Press.

———. 2012. *Human Development Report*. New York: Oxford University Press.

———. 2014. *Human Development Report*. New York: Oxford University Press.

UNESCO and UN Water. 2003. 'Water for People, Water for Life' (WWDR I). http://www.unesco.org/new/en/natural-sciences/environment/water/wwap/wwdr/wwdr1-2003/.

———. 2006. 'Water: A Shared Responsibility' (WWDR II). http://www.unesco.org/new/en/natural-sciences/environment/water/wwap/wwdr/wwdr2-2006/.

———. 2009. 'Water in a Changing World' (WWDR III). http://www.unesco.org/new/en/natural-sciences/environment/water/wwap/wwdr/wwdr3-2009/.

————. 2012. 'Managing Water under Uncertainty and Risk' (WWDR IV). http://www.unesco.org/new/en/natural-sciences/environment/water/wwap/wwdr/wwdr4-2012/.

UNFPA. 2007. 'State of the World's Population'. http://www.unfpa/org/swp/2007/index.htm.

Van der Zaag, P. 2005. 'Integrated Water Resources Management: Relevant Concept or Irrelevant Buzzword? A Capacity-building and Research Agenda for Southern Africa'. *Physics and Chemistry of the Earth* 30: 867–71.

Vanderpost, C. 2000. 'Putting the Bushmen on the Map of Botswana'. *Botswana Notes and Records* 32: 107–16.

WaterAid Tanzania. 2008. *Why did City Water Fail?* Dar es Salaam: WaterAid Tanzania.

Wolf, A., T. Shira, B. Yoffe and M. Giordano. 2003. 'International Waters: Identifying Basins at Risk'. *Water Policy* 5: 29–60.

Wolf, A.T., A. Kramer, A. Carius and G.D. Dabelko. 2005. *Managing Water Conflict and Cooperation: State of the World 2005 – Redefining Global Security*. Washington, D.C.: Worldwatch Institute.

Woodhouse, P. 2012. 'Foreign Agricultural Land Acquisition and the Visibility of Water Resource Impacts in Sub-Saharan Africa'. *Water Alternatives* 5(5): 208–22.

World Economic Forum (WEF). 2011. *Water Security: The Water-food-energy-climate Nexus*. Washington, D.C.: Island Press.

Young, O. 1969. 'Interdependencies in World Politics'. *International Journal* 24: 726–50.

Zeitoun, M. and J. Warner. 2006. 'Hydro-hegemony: A Framework for Analysis of Trans-boundary Water Conflicts'. *Water Policy* 8(5): 435–60.

Index